THE
INFLUENZA PANDEMIC
OF 1918-1919

GREAT HISTORIC DISASTERS

GREAT HISTORIC DISASTERS

THE INFLUENZA PANDEMIC OF 1918–1919

PAUL KUPPERBERG

CHELSEA HOUSE
PUBLISHERS

An imprint of Infobase Publishing

THE INFLUENZA PANDEMIC OF 1918–1919

Chelsea House
An imprint of Infobase Publishing
132 West 31st Street
New York NY 10001

Library of Congress Cataloging-in-Publication Data
Kupperberg, Paul.
The Influenza pandemic of 1918–1919/Paul Kupperberg.
   p. cm.—(Great historic disasters)
Includes bibliographical references and index.
ISBN: 978-0-7910-9640-6 (hardcover)
1. Influenza Epidemic, 1918–1919—Juvenile literature. I. Title. II. Series.
RC150.4.K87 2008
614.5'1809041—dc22   2007036552

Chelsea House books are available at special discounts when purchased in bulk quantities for businesses, associations, institutions, or sales promotions. Please call our Special Sales Department in New York at (212) 967-8800 or (800) 322-8755.

You can find Chelsea House on the World Wide Web
at http://www.chelseahouse.com

Text design by Annie O'Donnell
Cover design by Ben Peterson

Printed in the United States of America

Bang KT 10 9 8 7 6 5 4 3 2 1

This book is printed on acid-free paper.

All links and Web addresses were checked and verified to be correct at the time of publication. Because of the dynamic nature of the Web, some addresses and links may have changed since publication and may no longer be valid.

Contents

Introduction:
"Influenza of a Severe Type"

In 1855, the science of medicine was still struggling to gain acceptance amid thousands of years of healing knowledge based on well-meaning but faulty ideas of the nature and causes of disease. Many people believed that illness was caused by "miasma," or foul emanations from soil, air, and water. These emanations created an imbalance of what were known as the four "humors," or fluids: yellow bile (urine), black bile (feces), blood, and phlegm (saliva). Too much of one or not enough of another caused various health problems that doctors believed could be cured by, among other methods, inducing vomiting or bleeding the patient to restore harmony.

The true cause of illness, known as the germ theory of disease—which states that disease is caused by microorganisms that infect the body from outside through the air or through contact with infected individuals—was just beginning to gain acceptance in the medical community. It would not be until the last quarter of the nineteenth century, with the discovery of microorganisms as the true carriers of disease, that the old theories would finally be discarded.

But even with acceptance, few tried and true medicines existed to prevent or cure disease. Vaccination, which is the introduction of a small dose of disease into the body to force the body to develop disease-specific antibodies and immunity to that disease, had been proven successful by Dr. Edward Jenner (1749–1823) in Gloucestershire, England, against cowpox in 1796. The concept of sanitation and personal hygiene being connected to health was only beginning to gain traction; in 1854, Dr. John Snow (1813–1858) traced the source of an outbreak of cholera, an acute intestinal infection causing diarrhea and vomiting that can quickly lead to severe dehydration and death, to a single, infected public water pump on London's Broad Street. He deduced that the water was tainted; the pump was removed, and within three days, the spread of the outbreak halted.

Two decades later, Dr. Robert Koch (1843–1910), a German physician, proved that anthrax, a disease common to cattle, sheep, horses, and goats in the area in which he lived, was caused by the microorganism *Anthrax bacillus*, which had been discovered in 1850. This was the first time a disease had been linked to a specific bacterium, an idea that the French physician and research scientist Louis Pasteur (1822–1895) later expanded on in his research of the infectious disease rabies.

By the early decades of the twentieth century, medical science had left the old ideas behind. The *cause* of disease was understood, even if treatment was still beyond its means. Doctors, who half a century earlier might have moved from the dissection room to the operating theater without stopping to wash their hands, were now conscious of such hygienic practices as sterilization of medical instruments by high heat to kill microorganisms.

But, even by 1918, when Dr. Loring Miner, a recent graduate of Ohio University, saw the first cases of influenza in Haskell County, Kansas, the *treatment* of disease was still in its infancy. Doctors could diagnose an illness and try to make their patients comfortable, but there were precious few medications, including aspirin and morphine, to alleviate symptoms and fewer to actually cure diseases. So, when case after case of an unusually intense and rapidly progressing influenza struck, swiftly killing dozens of formerly strong and healthy patients, there was little this country doctor, though a progressive man of science, could do except study the killer.

Dr. Miner had, of course, seen outbreaks of influenza before but none as severe as this. He collected blood, urine, and sputum samples from his infected patients and scoured

In Lawrence, Massachusetts, in 1918, nurses care for victims of a Spanish influenza epidemic. The epidemic rapidly spread around the world, killing more than 100 million people.

medical literature for answers. Though the outbreak began to subside by March 1918, Dr. Miner's concerns did not. He wrote to the U.S. Public Health Service's weekly journal, *Public Health Reports*, to warn of "influenza of severe type," but his was the lone voice of warning on the possible outbreak of a virulent new strain of a deadly disease.

Since April 1917, the United States had been involved in the war then raging across Europe. Indeed, in expectation of entering the conflict, the country had been mobilizing, enacting the draft in May 1918 and building military camps and training facilities as fast as possible. Never before had so many men been brought together in such tightly confined quarters in so short an amount of time.

But as deadly as the European conflict was expected to be, there were those who knew of an even deadlier threat facing America's military forces, a threat responsible for more deaths during wartime than combat: disease. Among those sounding the warning were U.S. Army Surgeon General William Gorgas (1854–1920) and Dr. William Henry Welch (1850–1934), the influential head of Johns Hopkins University, the first modern medical school in America. Both men knew that, throughout history, not only had disease claimed more soldiers than had the wars they fought but also that disease routinely and swiftly spread from armies to civilian populations.

In spite of their records in the field of contagious diseases—Dr. Gorgas was responsible for implementing the sanitary conditions that halted the rampant spread of malaria in Panama and allowed for the completion of the Panama Canal at the turn of the century—their calls for measures to prevent the spread of disease among the growing army were given little governmental attention and even less support.

Thus, in early September 1918, the first cases of influenza (which, because it was first recognized and reported in Spain, became known as the Spanish flu) were being seen at Camp Devens, near Boston.

Dr. Miner had sounded the first warnings. But before the deadly disease could run its course in 1919, more American soldiers would die from the flu than in combat, more than one-fifth of the world's population would be infected, and as many as 100 million people worldwide would die from the disease that caused the most devastating pandemic in history.

The Influenzavirus

According to *Taber's Cyclopedic Medical Dictionary*, influenza is "an acute, contagious respiratory infection characterized by sudden onset, fever, chills, headaches, myalgia (muscle pain), and sometimes prostration. Coryza (head congestion and runny nose), cough and sore throat are common." As unpleasant as these symptoms can be, *Taber's* reports that influenza "ordinarily runs from four to five days . . . (and) as a rule, outcome is favorable in absence of pulmonary (lung-related) complications." In many cases, sufferers of influenza mistake their symptoms for those of the common cold and do not seek treatment beyond over-the-counter remedies that alleviate the discomfort of their symptoms.

While it is not known when influenza first appeared in the human population, scientists know that it began as an avian (bird) virus and then mutated (randomly and unexpectedly changed in genetic structure) to a form that enabled it to affect people. The Greek physician Hippocrates (460–370 B.C.), known as the father of modern medicine for his belief that illness came not from gods or evil spirits but from the patient, clearly described the symptoms of human influenza more than 2,400 years ago.

There have been repeated influenza pandemics (global epidemics) throughout history, but because its symptoms are similar to diseases such as typhoid fever, typhus, diphtheria, and others, it was not until A.D. 1580 that medical historians could confirm that an outbreak that spread across Asia, Africa, and Europe was influenza. More than 8,000 people died in Rome in this sixteenth-century outbreak, while the populations of several Spanish cities were almost wiped out. Sporadic pandemics throughout the seventeenth and eighteenth centuries claimed hundreds of thousands of victims.

Between 1830 and 1848, four major influenza epidemics struck China, Russia, and Europe, but these were of a more moderate strain of the disease that struck down mostly those with weakened or compromised immune systems, including the very young and the elderly.

Hippocrates, the founder of modern medicine, documented symptoms that resembled the flu around 412 B.C. His use of elderberries to treat influenza is still in practice today, and research is being done to test the treatment's effectiveness on bird flu.

HOW VIRUSES WORK

Viruses are microscopic organisms that enter living plant, animal, or bacterial cells and use the host cell's own chemical energy and genetic material to reproduce. The by-product of these parasites (an organism that feeds off another without benefiting or killing the host organism) infects and sickens the host cell, which, once it has been depleted of everything it has to offer the invading virus, dies. This releases newly produced virus particles that spread throughout the host system to continue the reproductive cycle.

Some viruses do not kill the host cells but instead transform them into cancerous states that cause uncontrolled cellular growth. Viruses are responsible for not only influenza but also human immunodeficiency virus (HIV), measles, mumps, yellow fever, poliomyelitis, and the common cold, and unlike bacterial infections, they do not respond to treatment with antibiotics.

Viruses are also unlike bacteria, which are single-celled organisms with a metabolism that require food, produce waste, and reproduce by dividing themselves. Viruses are not living organisms so much as they are collections of chemicals contained by a membrane. They perform no metabolic functions of their own and require a host organism to reproduce. And that is a virus's sole function: to reproduce. But because it contains none of the biological mechanisms to do this on its own, it must draw on the metabolisms of other organisms to do the job.

The surfaces of viruses contain chemically coded spikes and protuberances, and each type of virus has its own unique topography. When a virus invades a body, it collides with cells that the spikes and protuberances brush against. If the spikes encounter the proper receptor (the chemical "glove" that fits over the spikes' and protuberances' "hand"), the two organisms will bind. This process is known as adsorption (the adherence of the virus to the host cell).

The influenzavirus next creates an opening in the cell membrane through which it enters; many other kinds of viruses will adhere to the membrane's outer wall, but by entering the cell, the influenzavirus is able to hide from the body's immune system and thus avoids being found and killed before it can begin to reproduce.

The virus's genetic structure is encoded in its RNA (ribonucleic acid) as opposed to DNA (deoxyribonucleic acid), which is where the majority of life-forms keep their genetic code—much like a computer's programming code—that controls an organism's function and form. DNA and RNA are both strings of chemicals that combine in a variety of ways to create genes, the basic building blocks of all life. Each gene serves a specific function, determining everything from what type of plant or animal an organism will become to the color of a human's eyes or the size of a petal on a flower.

A virus gains control over cells by inserting genes into the host cell, which then direct the cell to perform functions that benefit the virus rather than the cell. Each virus will create thousands of bits of viral protein using the cell's biological functions. These will then bind with copies of the virus's genes to form new viruses, which eventually burst from the cell, killing it even as it sends anywhere from 100,000 to one million new viruses out to invade surrounding cells.

All of this takes place within hours of the start of the virus's attack in the warm, moist mucous membranes inside our mouth, nose, and throat. So every time we cough, sneeze, or exhale, we expel active viruses; we also transfer virus-laden bodily fluids to every surface we touch. We are infectious (capable of infecting others) for up to seven days after we are ourselves infected.

INFECTION, MUTATION, AND ANTIGENIC SHIFT

Influenza was named in fifteenth-century Italy, where the cause of the disease was blamed on unfavorable astrological "influences." That soon became *influenza di freddo*, or "influence of the cold," and the word made its way to the English-speaking world during a 1743 European outbreak. Influenza has also been known throughout history as epidemic catarrh, grippe (also grip or gripe), and the sweating sickness.

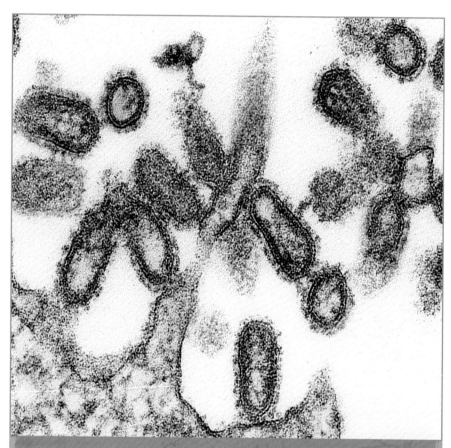

This image, taken with an electron microscope, shows a specimen that has qualities similar to the virus that caused the 1918 influenza pandemic. Because the flu virus's genetic characteristics shift so frequently, new flu vaccines are issued every year, and officials are on alert for new, stronger versions of influenza, such as Avian Influenza (Bird Flu).

Influenza is caused by viruses of the family Orthomyxo-viridae, which includes the influenzaviruses Isavirus and Thogotovirus.

The three types of influenza are known as Influenzavirus A, B, and C. Type A is the strain most likely to cause epidemics. Type B infects humans almost exclusively (the only other animal that can be infected by this strain is the seal) but is not responsible for epidemics. Types A and C are infectious in humans, birds, and pigs, although type C rarely causes disease in humans.

There are so many different strains of this single type of influenza because of its tendency to antigenic shift. Antigenic shift is what occurs when two different strains of influenza combine, forming a new subtype that contains a mixture of the antigens from the two original strains. Antigenic shift is seen only in influenza; the process in other viruses is known as reassortment or viral shift.

Influenzaviruses can also undergo a process called antigenic drift, which is a natural mutation that occurs over time and enables viruses to evade the immune system by changing into a form that existing antibodies cannot recognize. While antigenic drift occurs in all three types of the influenzavirus, antigenic shift is possible only in influenza A because that is the only strain that can infect other mammals and birds in addition to humans.

So, for example, pigs can be infected simultaneously with human and avian strains of influenza in addition to swine influenzaviruses, which can reassort, or mix, to produce a new virus containing genes from the human virus and hemagglutinin and/or neuraminidase from the avian virus. This new virus will be infectious to humans even though it contains a combination of surface proteins previously not seen in such viruses.

Because it has a built-in self-checking mechanism that eliminates most mutations before they can be passed on to an offspring, DNA is far more stable and reliable a conveyer

Type A Strains of Influenza

Type A influenzaviruses, which cause the most severe disease and are deadliest to humans, are composed of combinations of 16 different hemagglutinin subtypes and nine different neuraminidase subtypes, which are the proteins found on the influenzavirus's surface that allow it to bind to the host cell. Based on the combination of these proteins, type A has been subdivided into different serotypes (a group of closely related microorganisms distinguished by a characteristic set of antigens, or antibodies, their presence in the body triggers to fight off infection). These have been designated as:

* H1N1, also known as Spanish flu
* H2N2, or Asian flu
* H3N2, or Hong Kong flu
* H5N1, which is believed to have the potential to become pandemic in the 2007 flu season

of genetic information than RNA. Lacking this mechanism, viruses whose genes are carried by RNA are more likely to develop mutations and will mutate anywhere from 10,000 to one million times faster than a DNA virus. HIV, the virus that causes AIDS, and coronavirus (the cause of the common cold) are also fast-mutating RNA viruses.

While 99 percent of mutations in an RNA virus such as influenza destroy the virus's ability to infect other cells or kill it outright, the remaining one percent of viable mutations remain capable of performing their biological function.

* H7N, which has been shown to infect humans, birds, pigs, seals, horses, and laboratory mice, posing a higher-than-usual threat of pandemic

* H1N2, which is endemic (associated with particular locations or population groups) to humans and pigs

* H9N2, the subtype responsible for outbreaks of flu in both human and bird populations in Hong Kong in 1999 and 2003

* H7N2, a new subtype first seen in isolated cases in Virginia in 2002 and New York in 2003

* H7N3, a strain first seen in 1963 and last confirmed in poultry farms in British Columbia in 2004; its symptoms include conjunctivitis (pink eye) and mild flu symptoms

* H10N7, first seen in poultry on Minnesota turkey farms in 1979–1980; the first reported human cases of this strain were in Egypt in 2004

RESISTANCE AND IMMUNITY

Rather like the way a computer protects itself from infection by man-made programming "viruses" with antivirus programs that seek out and destroy the invading code, the human body also comes equipped with a sophisticated defense system. This is known as the immune system, and it begins at the body's protective barrier, the skin. Germs enter the body through the nose, mouth, and eyes, but our mucus, saliva, and tears all contain the antibacterial enzyme lysozyme that kills most bacteria by breaking down their cellular walls before they can enter our systems.

Any germ that makes it past these perimeter defenses must then pass through a host of internal defenses before it can unleash its pathogens (disease-causing organisms), beginning with the lymph system, a network that runs through our bodies. The system carries lymph, the liquid base of blood, which passes through a series of lymph nodes that detect and filter out invading bacteria.

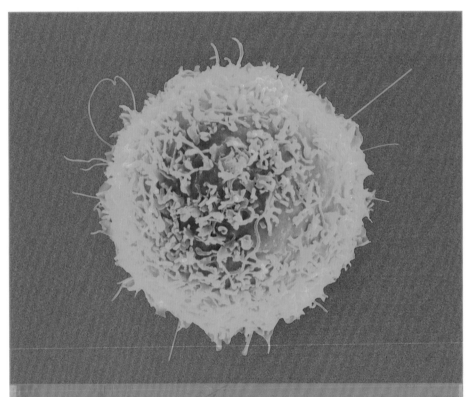

Lymphocytes are produced by the immune system, and eventually become either T or B cells, designed to attack body invaders such as bacteria and viruses. These cells, however, are slow to respond if they encounter an evolved virus, one that is similar to the original version of an already-beaten infection. Because of their slow reaction, these cells can be deadly if they cannot counter a fast-acting virus such as the one in the 1918 flu pandemic.

The thymus is a gland in the chest that produces T cells, the white blood cells that seek out and destroy viruses. The spleen filters the blood in search of foreign cells and old red blood cells in need of replacement, while the bone marrow produces new red and white blood cells as needed. Red blood cells carry oxygen throughout the body. White blood cells are the foot soldiers of the immune system. They are the antibodies, attracted to any foreign material, inflammation, or bacteria, engulfing it and destroying it with enzymes and chemicals.

Lymphocytes are also produced in the bone marrow and deal with most of the body's viral and bacterial infections in their forms as T cells or B cells, which mature into the plasma cells that produce antibodies. An antibody is a protein tuned to a particular germ that, when present, signals the B cell to clone itself and create millions of antibodies to destroy the bacteria.

The danger with mutations is that they create new forms of an old virus that the body's defense systems no longer recognize because of even a small change in the composition of the virus's proteins. This allows the mutated virus a chance to gain a foothold in the body before the immune system can develop the necessary T cells to find and destroy the invading pathogens.

So exposure to and survival of a particular strain of influenza gives us immunity to future infection by that same strain. But because of the rapidity of mutations in the influenzavirus, the exact strain of influenza (such as H1N1, H3N2, or H7N2) that strikes the general population changes from year to year. The trick today for medical researchers is to predict the particular strain that will strike in the upcoming flu season so that serotype-specific vaccines can be prepared in advance of the seasonal outbreak.

But in 1918, scientists had yet to achieve this greater understanding of the mechanics of viral infection or to develop vaccines to protect against them. They understood what caused disease and how it was transmitted through the air (via coughing and sneezing by an infected individual) or through infected surfaces (surfaces previously touched by infected individuals or their saliva or sputum). What they had yet to discover were successful ways to prevent the spread under the unusual and crowded conditions created by the nationwide mobilization for war or antiviral drugs to fight off or lessen the severity of disease.

America and the world were at war, but the real enemy was a mass invasion of an invisible foe, the influenzavirus.

2 Outbreak

I n Dr. Loring Miner's Haskell County, Kansas, practice, the first signs of what would prove to be the deadliest influenza pandemic in history began as several isolated cases in late January and February 1918. Patients presented with common, if unusually severe, influenza symptoms, including headaches and body aches, coughs, and high fevers. In keeping with the severity of infection, this influenza progressed in a matter of hours or days through patients, moving from first symptoms to severe illness or, in dozens of cases, death.

Also unusual was the fact that this influenza struck not just the very young, very old, or the weak (as was the common course of infection among a population) but seemed to target the strongest and healthiest of his patients. And it killed. Dr. Miner believed he was dealing with a new type of influenza. He sent out inquiries and warnings to colleagues and public health officials. He began to keep records and medical samples taken from his stricken patients and spent long hours in the laboratory trying to understand, and perhaps even combat, the invisible foe he faced.

The U.S. Public Health Service disregarded his reports, and patients continued to die until mid-March 1918, when as if a switch had been thrown, there were no new influenza reports in the United States or abroad. Haskell County's last few patients recovered, and the local outbreak seemed to be over.

Dr. Miner knew better. Even within the sparsely populated rural county, the disease had managed to make rapid progress. But anyone passing through the stricken area could easily have picked up the infection and been long gone before showing symptoms.

This danger was magnified by the great upheaval in population caused by the war, with millions of young soldiers crisscrossing the country, moving from often rural homes (the majority of Americans still lived in the countryside) to overcrowded military training camps, then to likely even more crowded ships that transported them to Europe, and finally, into closely quartered front-line units subjected to harsh, unsanitary conditions. The situation was perfect for the spread of this influenza. Precautions had to be taken.

No one but Dr. Miner seemed to be concerned.

CAMP FUNSTON, KANSAS

Three hundred miles from Haskell County was Camp Funston, located on the Fort Riley military reservation in Kansas. Hurriedly erected in 1917 as a training camp for military recruits, the camp was home to 56,000 troops from around the country. It was the second-largest military base in America, and conditions were hardly ideal in the record cold winter of 1917–1918: Barracks and tents were overcrowded and under heated, and warm clothing was scarce.

In the last half of February 1918, during the height of the Haskell County outbreak, two soldiers from Camp Funston were exposed to the influenza, one on a visit home, the second from a visiting relative. A third young man from Haskell

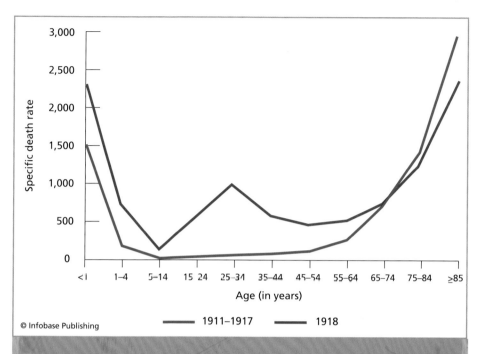

This graph depicts the sharp change in the flu virus within one year. The blue line shows that the influenza from 1911 to 1917 remained relatively similar to flu viruses of the past, only taking the lives of its youngest and oldest victims. The red line, however, represents those who died from the 1918 influenza pandemic, when a mutated flu virus managed to knock down the strongest and healthiest people.

County left home to report to Camp Funston at the end of the month.

The first reports of influenza at the camp came on March 4, 1918. Among those first afflicted was the camp cook, who could potentially have passed the disease on to every other man in the camp. By the end of the month, more than 1,100 men had been admitted to the hospital, with countless more receiving treatment at the infirmary. Almost 20 percent of the 237 who developed pneumonia (congestion and infection of the lungs) died.

Some influential people had tried hard to prepare for the outbreak of disease related to the overcrowded conditions. As members of the National Academy of Science, men such as Dr. William Henry Welch of Johns Hopkins University; Dr. Victor Vaughn, former dean of the School of Medicine at the University of Michigan and acting surgeon general of the U.S. Army; Charles (1898–1968) and William (1861–1939) Mayo, cofounders, with their father, of the cutting-edge Mayo Clinic in Rochester, Minnesota; and Dr. Hermann Biggs (1859–1923), the innovative head of the New York City Department of Health and a pioneer in the prevention and spread of disease, pressed for more rigorous standards of hygiene and public health.

The overcrowded conditions in camps across America meant the government was already ignoring its own regulations on space requirements and housing conditions for military personnel. The crush to process recruits through basic training so they could be shipped to the fierce fighting in France overwhelmed all other concerns.

These physicians understood a simple reality that politicians and generals overlooked: Disease was far deadlier a foe than any army ever raised by man. This was as true in ancient times as it was then. Disease claimed 10 British lives for every battlefield death in the Boer War (1899–1902); it took 2 lives for every 1 in the American Civil War (1861–1865), and the ratio was 6 to 1 in the Spanish-American War (1898).

Surgeon General Gorgas in particular understood what was at stake; he had been in Cuba right after the Spanish-American War and had also witnessed firsthand the effects of yellow fever on the workers in the Panama Canal Zone. Gorgas was a recognized expert on public health and sanitation and was one of the men who had helped find the causes of and helped stop the yellow fever epidemic. But the Department of War (as the Department of Defense was then called) was focused on the mobilization of men and equipment. Doctors, were responsible for taking care of whatever health problems arose. At first they were in short supply—at the start of the war, there were fewer than 800 doctors in the army and navy, but by war's end, more than 38,000 were serving, creating a shortage of doctors in the civilian population.

Like the others, Dr. Gorgas's warnings and protests fell on deaf ears.

ISOLATED OUTBREAKS AND A BRIEF LULL

An epidemic is a matter of numbers. One person infects two others, who in turn infect another two, who will each infect another two, and so on, until the infection has spread across the population. World War I made the spread of the influenza outbreak a foregone conclusion. Camp Funston saw a steady stream of men through its gates on their way to other bases or deployment in France.

A private at Fort Riley, reported to the infirmary with flu-like symptoms on the morning of March 11, 1918. By noon, 100 more were sick; by the weekend, influenza patients numbered 500.

On March 18, 1918, influenza made its appearance in Georgia at camps Forrest and Greenleaf. By the end of the spring, two-thirds of America's military bases experienced a more severe than usual outbreak of influenza. More than 30 U.S. cities, most of them located near major military bases, also saw an upswing in deaths due to influenza, but the numbers were not so high as to cause alarm.

And then, during the early summer months, the outbreak in the United States abated, a seeming repeat of the severe outbreak pattern in Haskell County. The disease had already shown up in Europe and swept across that continent, through the Mediterranean, and into Africa and the Far East. The American physicians concerned with stopping the spread of disease knew that as long as this particularly virulent strain of influenza remained active anywhere in the vicinity of American troops, the United States was still at risk.

Several local episodes throughout the summer of 1918 caused great concern, as on June 30, 1918, when a British freighter with an infected crew docked at a Philadelphia port. Doctors worked quickly, transporting the dozens of infected crewmen to a sealed ward in the local hospital. Many of the men died, most from pneumonia, but the disease did not spread.

By August, it was becoming more difficult to keep the influenza from jumping with full force back onto American shores. A ship en route to New York from France was so hard hit by the disease that it had to stop at Halifax, Nova Scotia,

Colonel W.C. Gorgas *(left)* was the U.S. Surgeon General just before the flu pandemic. Despite Gorgas's experience in preventing outbreaks of malaria and yellow fever by upholding sanitation standards, U.S. authorities were more concerned about World War I than his warnings on the spread of influenza.

The Symptoms of Influenza

Not everyone reacts the same way to influenza. Some experience minor discomfort, similar to a common cold, while others fall more severely ill.

The elderly, the young, and those with certain medical conditions and compromised immune systems are more likely to catch influenza and are at a higher risk for serious complications.

Depending on the strain of influenza, it can take a few hours or several days after a person is exposed to the virus (usually from respiratory droplets expelled on the coughs and sneezes of infected individuals) for symptoms to appear. After a person is infected, he or she is contagious—able to pass the disease on to others—for a day before the appearance of symptoms and up to five days after he or she becomes sick.

The symptoms of the common flu include a fever (which can be high), headache, fatigue, cough, and sore throat, as well as a stuffy or drippy nose, body aches, and diarrhea and vomiting, although those last two symptoms are more common in children than they are in adults.

The symptoms of common strains of influenza linger from three to five days, after which most patients recover. However, it can exacerbate, or worsen, certain chronic medical problems such as congestive heart failure, asthma, or diabetes, and complications can quickly arise, including dehydration, bacterial pneumonia, and a host of opportunistic infections taking advantage of weakened immune systems.

(continues)

(continued)

In the 1918–1919 pandemic, many patients suffered from cyanosis, a condition caused by pneumonia that leads to a lack of oxygen in the blood, which in turn causes bluish discoloration of the skin. This usually preceded a patient's death from restricted bloodflow.

Also common during the pandemic was a viral pneumonia that caused bleeding in the lungs, as well as bleeding from the nose, eyes, and ears. Still others suffered from bleeding beneath the skin, which caused black blotches that led many to believe the disease was bubonic plague rather than influenza.

During most years, influenza will infect approximately 20 percent of the population and cause an average of 36,000 deaths a year, but most people will suffer only the mild common symptoms and recover in days.

until enough of the crew recovered to continue on to the final destination. On August 12, a freighter from Norway docked at a Brooklyn, New York, pier after burying four dead from influenza at sea.

In the days that followed, several more ships arrived in New York carrying stricken crews. By August 20, the New York Department of Health was reporting that influenza was back in the city.

BOSTON'S COMMONWEALTH PIER AND CAMP DEVENS

The Navy's Commonwealth Pier in Boston was a temporary barracks that housed up to 7,000 sailors in transit from one posting to another. As with the country's army bases, the pier was overcrowded. It saw its first 2 cases of influenza on

August 27, followed by 8 more the next day and 58 more the day after that.

A pair of doctors at the Chelsea Naval Hospital where the influenza victims had been quickly transferred to, recognized what they were up against and worked quickly to isolate the patients and contain the spread of infection by trying to track down and isolate everyone with whom the patients had come into contact. The disease, however, was now presenting its symptoms, sickening and killing victims within 24 to 48 hours and spreading too fast for the doctors' efforts to be effective.

On September 3, a civilian was admitted to Boston City Hospital, and the next day, cases were reported at Harvard University. And at Camp Devens, a base just west of Boston, built to house 36,000 men but which now held 45,000, the first reported cases of influenza came in late August, with almost 30 new cases by the end of the month, all of which, because of the severity of the symptoms, had been misdiagnosed as pneumonia.

Beginning around the second week of September, the disease began to show itself with more and more frequency in the Boston area, both on and off military installations. With no reason to expect anything but a usual influenza season, public health officials and doctors failed to link these seemingly isolated pockets of disease with the overcrowding and constant movement of military personnel. It was a ticking bomb that, as one army report later stated, "occurred as an explosion."

Dr. Vaughn, the acting surgeon general of the army, was sent immediately to Camp Devens, which by his arrival was more a containment for the sick than a cantonment (temporary quarters) for soldiers. He came on a day when 63 men died. He later wrote in his report on the visit, "Every bed was full, yet others crowded in. The faces wore a bluish cast; a cough brought up the blood-stained sputum. In the morning, the dead bodies are stacked about the morgue like cordwood."

The explosion was terrible. On one day alone, 1,543 soldiers at the camp reported sick. By September 22, almost 20 percent of the camp was ill, and pneumonia quickly set in, affecting 342 men on September 24. Within days, because literally hundreds of civilian and military doctors and nurses were working around the clock to treat patients, the camp's medical staff began to fall victim to the epidemic. They were overwhelmed and were forced to close the hospital to any new patients.

Authorities were becoming aware of the dire nature of the situation. The Massachusetts State Health Department

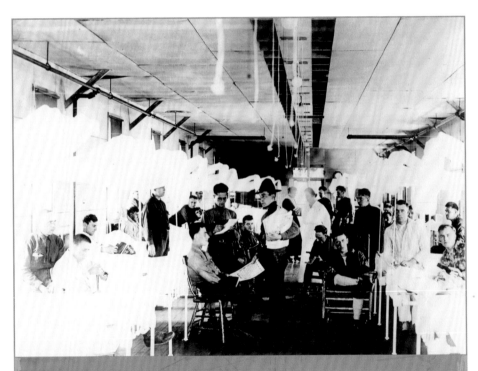

This picture of a hospital room shows the medical staff and patients at Fort Devens, one of the military bases that was consumed by the Spanish Flu. A letter written by a doctor working at Fort Devens during the pandemic describes soldiers checking into the infirmary with minor flu symptoms and quickly declining. Within a few hours, they were dead.

warned that "unless precautions are taken the disease in all probability will spread to the civilian population of (Boston)." On September 5, the department alerted local newspapers of the epidemic.

Dr. Roy Grist, one of the Camp Devens army doctors, wrote in a letter to a colleague that a patient brought in with an ordinary attack of influenza will "very rapidly develop the most vicious type of pneumonia that has ever been seen. Two hours after admission they have the Mahogany spots over the cheek bones, and a few hours later you can begin to see the Cyanosis extending from their ears and spreading all over the face, until it is hard to distinguish the coloured men from the white. It is only a matter of a few hours then until death comes... It is horrible." They were seeing, on average, 100 deaths a day, requiring special trains to take away the bodies.

"It beats any sight they ever had in France after a battle," Dr. Grist wrote. "An extra long barracks has been vacated for the use of the Morgue and it would make any man sit up and take notice to walk down the long lines of dead soldiers all dressed and laid out in double rows."

THE EXPLOSION

The infection continued playing its number game, each case leading to more cases that lead to more cases, multiplying into an epidemic and, by now, spreading too wide to contain or prevent.

From Camp Funston to Commonwealth Pier and Camp Devens, out into the civilian population through casual contact or family members, into military installations far and wide, the influenza was spreading rapidly. Sailors who had passed through Commonwealth Pier brought the infection to New Orleans on a ship that continued on to Mexico. Three hundred sailors from Boston arrived at the Philadelphia Navy Yard on September 7, and were reassigned to other units, many of which transferred to Puget Sound in Washington State.

Others from Boston shipped out to Chicago's Great Lakes Naval Training Station, the largest naval training facility in the country.

Sailors began falling ill at the Newport Naval Base in Rhode Island and at Camp Grant, outside of Rockford, Illinois. Even as soldiers began to die, more than 3,000 troops shipped out to Camp Hancock, Georgia. Their train arrived with one-quarter of the men on board ill. Eventually, two-thirds of those 3,000 would be hospitalized with at least 10 percent of them dying. In one day, 2,800 soldiers reported sick at Camp Custer, Michigan.

Overwhelmed with grief and helplessness at the scope of the tragedy and his own failure to do anything about the conditions that fostered the outbreak of more than 5,000 ill and killed 500 of his young troops, Camp Grant's commander, Colonel Charles Hagadorn, took his own life.

But this was only the first wave in the pandemic. The spread of this deadly virus was just beginning. The real horrors it would unleash to almost every corner of the globe were still to come.

3 Historic Pandemics and Epidemics

Even before the war in Europe began, a number of public health officials knew that disease would be a far greater threat than enemy bullets and bombs. History was full of reports of epidemics and pandemics that eradicated tens and hundreds of thousands, even millions, of people at a time, but the lessons of history were ignored for the needs of the present.

Any disease can become an epidemic, and as history shows, humanity has been hit with everything, including cholera, smallpox, measles, mumps, diphtheria, malaria, yellow fever, typhus, scarlet fever, typhoid, German measles, polio, HIV/AIDS, and many others.

EARLY PLAGUES

Among the earliest plagues, or epidemic diseases with a high death rate, on record occurred during the Peloponnesian War (431–404 B.C.) between Athens and Sparta, and was recorded by Athenian general and historian Thucydides (460–400 B.C.) in his *History of the Peloponnesian War*. Thucydides was himself a victim of the plague and, as a realistic writer who attributed events not to the gods but to human nature, was in a unique position to

Great Greek thinkers like Hippocrates and Thucydides moved away from common thought of the day and spurned the gods in favor of science and theory. Thucydides *(above)*, a Greek historian, survived a plague that swept through Athens and managed to document the symptoms and describe the situation in the city. Experts now believe Athenians were struck with a deadly strain of influenza along with toxic shock syndrome, a rare bacterial infection.

describe the symptoms and progress of the disease, which originated in Ethiopia before spreading to Egypt and Greece.

The initial symptoms included headache, conjunctivitis (pink eye), a full-body rash, and fever. Sufferers then
experienced painful stomach cramps and began coughing
up blood. They also had an unquenchable thirst that led
many to throw themselves into wells, further spreading the
contamination through the water. Those who did not die
from the disease by the end of a week would be stricken
with uncontrollable and often fatal diarrhea. Finally, even
those who did survive might suffer from permanent partial
paralysis, blindness, or amnesia.

Like the later twentieth-century influenza outbreak, the
Peloponnesian War plague managed to gain a hold on the
population because of the overcrowded wartime conditions of
Athens. Unlike that modern outbreak, no one is certain exactly
what disease caused this 2,500-year-old plague. Some experts
believe it might have been smallpox, while others think it was
a form of measles. Whatever it was, it killed tens of thousands
in Athens alone, including Pericles, former leader of Athens.

Strangely, the disease never affected the Spartans besieg-
ing the city; it only sickened those inside the walls of the city
who were spreading the contagion through unavoidable contact and unsanitary conditions.

Few such early historic events are fortunate enough to have
had witnesses as vivid and reliable as Thucydides. Most thinkers and scholars of those times attributed all disasters, big and
small, to the whims of the gods. A plague was a warning or
punishment sent from above, its symptoms and fatality rate a
matter of interpretation for the survivors.

BUBONIC PLAGUE

A writer whose work has survived into our time, Marcus Aurelius (A.D. 121–180), emperor of Rome and author of *Meditations*,
a memoir of his life in public service, was a plague victim who

did not survive to write of the experience. Aurelius holds a place in the history of medicine for having appointed as his personal physician Galen (A.D. 130–200). Galen began practicing medicine when tending to gladiators, which offered him a unique opportunity to view the inner workings of the human body through the often fatal wounds these men suffered. He would revolutionize medicine with numerous surgical techniques, and his writings would be sacred text for physicians in the Western world for centuries to come.

The disease that killed Emperor Aurelius was carried by his armies returning from Seleucia, a city on the banks of the Tigris River in northern Syria. It spread across Asia Minor, Egypt, Greece, and Italy, killing as much as one-third of the populations of some areas. There is some speculation that it was the bubonic plague, a disease common to rodents and caused by the bacterium *Yersinia pestis*.

Bubonic plague passes from rodent to human either through direct contact, such as a rat bite, or through an intermediary, usually a flea that has fed on the infected animal. Symptoms appear three to seven days after infection, beginning with chills, fever, headache, diarrhea, and swelling of the lymph nodes, where the bacteria replicate. The mortality rate of the plague if left untreated is about 10 percent.

Septicemic plague is even deadlier and causes internal bleeding and black patches on the skin; it is almost always fatal. Pneumonic plague, which infects the lungs, causes death in 95 percent of its victims. Of course, with modern antibiotics, bubonic and pneumonic plague are both treatable, while even with treatment, septicemic plague remains fatal in approximately 15 percent of cases.

The bubonic plague's most famous outbreak was the so-called Black Death of A.D. 1347–1351, a pandemic that claimed one-third of the population of Europe and as many as 75 million deaths worldwide. Following a series of outbreaks and epidemics of plague in India and the Chinese and Mongol empires, the plague traveled along land and sea trade routes to infect most of the known world.

Victims suffered horribly, dying in agony. Bodies were unceremoniously dumped onto streets to be collected by those still well enough to work. Entire nations ground to a halt as people were afraid to gather for pleasure or business for fear of catching the disease. In the Christian world, the plague was interpreted as divine punishment, but clergy and physicians died alongside thieves and killers.

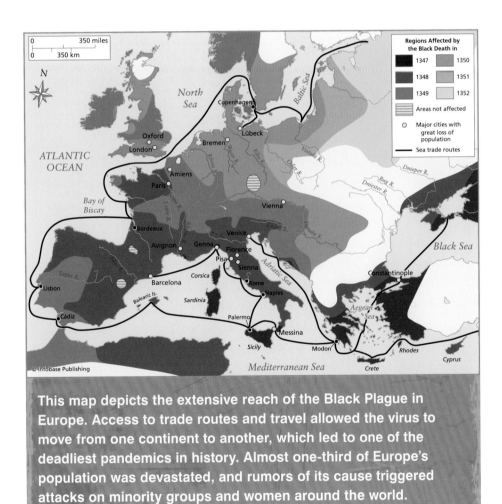

This map depicts the extensive reach of the Black Plague in Europe. Access to trade routes and travel allowed the virus to move from one continent to another, which led to one of the deadliest pandemics in history. Almost one-third of Europe's population was devastated, and rumors of its cause triggered attacks on minority groups and women around the world.

The plague remained a threat to Europe and the Mediterranean until the seventeenth century. It appeared seemingly without rhyme or reason and spread rapidly, as happened in England in numerous outbreaks between 1539 and 1566. Unfortunately, it would be centuries until science made the connection between rats, sanitation (to cut down on the rat population), and fleabites.

The last great European outbreak of this brutal disease was in London in 1666, after which it is speculated that the rat population was destroyed in that year's Great Fire, which consumed most of the city.

THE SPREAD OF AN EPIDEMIC

Ever since the first historically confirmed influenza outbreak in Europe, Asia, and Africa in A.D. 1580, the disease has been a periodic visitor in epidemic form and remains (in spite of the widespread availability of the influenza vaccine) a yearly killer, responsible for an estimated 36,000 deaths a year in the United States alone and many millions more the world over.

Epidemiology is the study of public health and the factors that affect it. Epidemiologists use scientific analysis, experimentation, and statistical evidence to study everything from how disease starts and spreads to methods of prevention and even cures. It is forensic medicine that interprets and establishes the facts of disease.

One of the earliest epidemiologists was Dr. John Snow, the London physician who traced an 1854 cholera outbreak to a single tainted pump. In the last week of August, residents of an area of London known as Golden Square took ill and began dying. Hundreds of victims were stricken within hours, many within five square blocks of this poor neighborhood.

London was no stranger to cholera, having suffered through earlier outbreaks in the 1830s and 1840s, one of which killed almost 7,500 Londoners in two years. What was unknown to them was the cause of the disease. Most believed all illnesses were carried through the air as a miasma, or a vapor, like a poisonous smell. Dr. Snow, a private physician with experience treating cholera as an apprentice during an earlier outbreak, thought that the truth of the matter lay with the germ theory of disease and went in search of the contagion.

Dr. Snow conducted an exhaustive examination of the outbreak, checking water samples under the microscope, studying the death statistics, and looking for geographical patterns that would lead him to the outbreak's point of origin. He used a map to chart the cases, which led, finally, to a public water pump on Broad Street. The city's Board of Governors heard

John Snow, one of the world's first epidemiologists, literally became a virus hunter when he used detective skills to map out cases and zone in on a contaminated water pump that was causing a cholera outbreak in London.

Snow's testimony and ordered the suspect pump shut down and, within days, no new cases were appearing. It was later learned that the water was contaminated by a sick baby's diapers that had been washed at the well.

Of course, the bacteria that actually caused the disease would not be identified for some 30 more years, but if nothing

Influenza Outbreaks in History

1580: Beginning in Asia, this pandemic spread across Africa, Europe, and America, afflicting 90 percent of the population of some areas and bringing high mortality rates. The main treatment in Europe was to bleed patients.

18th century: Three major pandemics occurred in 1729–1730, 1732–1733, and 1781–1782. The deadliest was the 1781 outbreak, which began in Asia and spread rapidly across Russia and Europe, killing mostly the elderly.

19th century: This century also saw a trio of pandemics, in 1830–1831, 1833–1834, and 1889–1890. The final outbreak, known as the Russian flu, spread through Europe and reached North America in 1890.

1850–1851: An outbreak that swept through North and South America, the West Indies, Australia, and Germany.

1889–1900: Believed to have begun in Russia, this pandemic—known as the Asiatic influenza—exploded across western Europe, North and South America, the eastern Mediterranean, and into India. It is the worst else, Dr. Snow had established a link between public sanitation, contamination, and the spread of disease. Others would follow his lead and, within decades, the helplessness that public health officials had felt in the face of "miasmic" diseases was replaced by the knowledge that what caused disease was something that could be hunted down and, in some cases, even eliminated.

of the nineteenth-century pandemics, and the strain reappeared in epidemics over subsequent years.

1918–1919: The Spanish influenza pandemic.

1924: The first outbreak of bird flu, or HPAI avian influenza, was reported in the United States. It did not spread to humans.

1957–1958: Beginning in China, the Asian flu (H2N2) was the century's second worst pandemic, killing one million worldwide, including 70,000 Americans.

1976: Swine flu was reported at the Fort Dix, New Jersey, military base, killing one before it was contained. Health officials initially feared it was Spanish flu, the same strain (H1N1) that caused the 1918–1919 pandemic,

1983: Seventeen million birds, including chickens, turkeys, and guinea fowl, in Pennsylvania and Virginia were destroyed in order to control the outbreak of an H5N2 virus and prevent its spread among humans.

1997: A strain of bird flu (H5N1) that had been epidemic among birds in Hong Kong passes to a human, who died. In November and December, 18 new cases of H5N1 were reported, a dozen from direct contact with infected poultry. Six people died, and 1.4 million chickens and ducks were destroyed.

DETECTIVE WORK

As we have seen, disease can be spread in several ways: by contact with an infected person's blood or saliva, usually by being coughed or sneezed upon; by exposure to contaminated water or food, usually laced with fecal matter; from a "middle-man," such as the fleas from rats infected with bubonic plague; or even, as in the case of malaria, from an insect carrying the disease itself.

Malaria (a word coined in medieval Italy that means "bad air") is another great killer that is still widespread in tropical and subtropical regions. Approximately 400 million people are infected every year, resulting in between 1 million and 3 million deaths, but because so many of these deaths occur in poverty-stricken areas such as sub-Saharan Africa, accurate statistics are impossible to establish.

Malaria causes fever, vomiting, chills, joint pain, and convulsions. It can also cause brain damage in young children, as well as severe, often fatal, anemia (a condition that occurs when there is an abnormal reduction of red blood cells, depriving the body of the oxygen the cells carry). The parasites that cause the disease have been around for as long as humans have existed, and close genetic relatives of the human malaria parasite can still be found in our closest genetic relatives, chimpanzees. The earliest recorded malaria outbreak was in China in 2700 B.C., and humanity was still dealing with the disease at the turn of the twentieth century.

Malaria had always been a problem for people in tropical climates, something the European and American colonizers of India, Africa, and South and Central America quickly learned.

The parasite behind malaria was discovered in 1880 by Charles-Louis-Alphonse Laveran (1845–1922), a French army doctor stationed in Algeria. He observed the protozoan (single-celled animal) in the blood of malaria patients and concluded it was the cause, the first time a protozoan was identified as a pathogen.

In 1881, Cuban doctor Carlos Finlay (1833–1915), who was treating yellow fever in Havana, proposed that this disease was carried and transmitted by mosquitoes, but this theory was not tested until 1897, when Sir Ronald Ross (1857–1932), stationed in India, made the connection between access to water and the breeding cycles of mosquitoes. By minimizing the presence of the standing, stagnant water that mosquitoes require to breed, Dr. Ross determined that the constant infestation of these pesky tropical insects could be controlled.

Continuing his interest in mosquitoes, Dr. Ross later found the presence of the malarial parasite in the *Anopheles*, a species of mosquito. After feeding a healthy mosquito blood from a

A South American malaria vector mosquito *(Anophiles albimanus)* feeds on a human arm *(above)*. Sir Ronald Ross studied the patterns of mosquitoes and found that occurrences of malaria could be controlled by increasing sanitation efforts.

malarial patient, he saw that the pest picked up the parasite, and using birds as test subjects, he proved that the disease was passed from bird to bird by the bite of infected mosquitoes.

In 1900, America was in the process of building the canal across the isthmus of Panama in Central America. The relatively narrow strip of land was all that separated the Atlantic and Pacific Oceans, and a canal, which would shorten the voyage between New York and San Francisco from 14,000 miles (22,500 kilometers [km]) to 6,000 miles (9,500 km), was of vital strategic and economic importance to the United States.

Unfortunately, the tropical area was infested with mosquitoes. Walter Reed (1851–1902) was an army doctor who specialized in infectious disease. He had studied the 1899 Cuban yellow fever outbreak and disproved the widespread belief that the disease was spread by clothing and bedding soiled by the excrement (feces) of the ill. He concluded that the fever was passed by mosquitoes, and because there was no treatment for yellow fever, Reed and his team of epidemiologists set about cleaning up the standing water that was the breeding ground for the carriers.

Now, Dr. Reed was sent to study the situation in Panama, where as many as 27,500 workers would die—most from diseases such as malaria and yellow fever—before his work was done. After deliberately exposing themselves to mosquitoes known to be infected with malaria, researchers determined that, as in Cuba, the culprit was the mosquito, and the solution was a massive public sanitation effort.

Following this detective-like approach to science, researchers continue to delve into the mysteries of science and disease. While once epidemic diseases such as smallpox, tuberculosis, polio, and measles can now be effectively eradicated through vaccination, and cholera, diphtheria, and yellow fever controlled through sanitation. However, there is still little that can be done—beyond quick action in containing new strains of a disease, as has been done in recent years—to prevent a new epidemic strain of influenza from spreading.

Each year brings the possibility of new strains of the virus, any one of which might be a mutation that spreads the disease around the world in spite of vaccines and other preventive measures. Because pandemics of any disease are, by nature, fast moving and adaptive, the best that can be done is to isolate patients, prevent situations favorable for the spread of a pathogen, treat those that can be saved, and provide comfort to those that cannot. The disease, once unleashed, has a numerical destiny and will not be stopped until it has run its course.

4. North America

Mathematicians have devised formulas that predict the speed and rate of infection among populations. Parts of this formula take the number of infected and use it to predict the number of people who have not yet taken ill but are susceptible to infection. At the other end of the equation are those who, once infected, either die or recover with an immunity to reinfection by that same strain of the virus.

The number to watch is the number of susceptible victims—those living in crowded or unsanitary conditions, individuals with low or compromised immunity systems, the elderly, infants, etc.—because, until the disease runs through that population, there are still those capable of catching and continuing the disease.

The numbers were beginning to multiply faster than the human agencies combating influenza could contend with the disease. Conditions in the United States could not have been more condusive for the pandemic spread of this particular strain of influenza. In this case, not only was a substantial portion of the country on the move because of the war, but this strain of influenza even targeted the young and healthy, the very population that made up the mass of mobile young recruits moving from one overcrowded military base to another.

NEW YORK

Not surprisingly, cities were hit early and hard by influenza. Many were located near major military encampments or were important hubs of rail and sea transportation. They were, by their very nature, densely packed, dirty, and full of very poor people who tended to live in bad conditions.

The first influenza death in New York City was on September 15, 1918. The city's piers had seen the coming and going of countless ships to and from the fighting in Europe, and the influenzavirus worked swiftly in the ideal climate of one of the most densely packed cities in the world.

Royal Copeland (1868–1938), the city's health commissioner, did nothing, announcing to the press: "The city is in no danger of an epidemic. No need for our people to worry." A political appointee without a medical degree, he at first denied that Spanish influenza was the cause of all the reported illnesses, then relented and ordered all victims to be quarantined.

As the epidemic ran its numeric course, literally hundreds of thousands of people were sick at any given time. In one hospital, a doctor found all new patients occupying the critical care unit every morning, replacing the previous day's roster that had died overnight.

Ships from Europe, itself aflame with Spanish influenza, continued to dock in New York. Assistant Secretary of the Navy and future four-time president of the United States Franklin Delano Roosevelt (1882–1945) contracted influenza. He remained deathly ill and confined to bed for two weeks.

More than 850 New Yorkers died on a single day in mid-October, and by the time the worst was over, the total number of dead in the city would exceed 35,000.

PHILADELPHIA

On September 28, 1918, Philadelphia, Pennsylvania, hosted the Fourth Liberty Loan parade to support the war through the sale of war bonds. An estimated 200,000 people attended, and by October 1, 635 new cases of influenza were reported as a result. City officials acknowledged in a statement from the

U.S. Deaths from Influenza

Complete records of U.S. infections and deaths from the 1918–1919 pandemic will never be known. Due to a large rural population, less sophisticated recordkeeping, and many patients who suffered through the disease without ever seeing a doctor, those statistics can never be accurately compiled.

The first cases were reported in Arkansas on October 4, 1918. Within one week, a state report indicated that "serious epidemics have been reported from several points," and within two weeks, there was an average of 1,800 new cases reported daily.

Influenza struck California at the end of September 1918 in Belvedere, San Gabriel, and Los Angeles. Though initially optimistic about containing the outbreak (in Los Angeles, health officials announced: "There is no cause for alarm"), schools, churches, and other places of public gathering were soon closed, and many communities made it mandatory to wear face masks. By the beginning of November, there were more than 115,000 reported cases and deaths across the state.

The nation's capital was not spared. Influenza struck in late September, and within two weeks, thousands had sickened.

health commissioner that this epidemic among civilians "was assuming the type found in naval stations and cantonments."

This was the Spanish influenza, quick to spread and just as quick to produce symptoms. As people got sick, schools, churches, theaters, and all other places of "public amusement" were ordered closed.

The next week saw 440 new victims, with more than 730 the week after that.

In Idaho's Franklin County, about 1,300 of the county's 8,000 residents were taken ill, 31 of whom died. The town of Paris suffered an almost 50 percent mortality rate.

Infected troops passing through Kentucky brought the disease to that state in September 1918. Louisville experienced almost 1,000 cases in the first week alone, with about 180 deaths in each of the next several weeks. Statewide, thousands of cases were being diagnosed every week, one coal miner reporting that "every porch that I'd look at . . . would have a casket box a sittin' on it." The mines were closed for six weeks.

In Virginia, more than 200,000 cases of influenza were reported by mid-October. By the end of 1918, more than 15,000 Virginians died.

Overwhelmed with the sick and dying, health officials in Montana were unable to report their numbers until the last week in October, at which time there had been more than 3,500 cases. Admitting their reports were "very incomplete," officials on November 1 said that at least 11,500 people had become ill in the previous 3 weeks.

That did little to stem the rapid spread. Every bed in the city's 31 hospitals was filled, forcing people to wait in long, hopeless lines for medical help or, if they had the strength, return home. There was, at any rate, no medicine available for what ailed them. A hastily erected emergency hospital (the first of two that would be built) filled its 500 beds in a day, and still people died daily by the hundreds.

People who spit in public were arrested. Signs warned the population to use a handkerchief when coughing or sneezing and to avoid crowds. Health and city workers wore face masks

Policemen in Seattle wear face masks while working in public. As one of the most effective preventative measures against influenza, people across America wore the masks, and those who did not were denied access to public services, such as transportation. Some municipalities even declared it illegal to shake hands.

at all times, yet doctors were sickening and dying at a rate equal to the civilian populations.

On October 5, 254 people died; 289 died the next day; more than 300 the two days after that, and on October 9, 428. The horrifying numbers kept climbing. There seemed to be no end in sight.

The city could not handle the staggering number of dead. The supply of coffins quickly ran out. Bodies were wrapped in sheets and left where the people died as public facilities were overwhelmed; the city morgue had room for 36 bodies and was storing 200. Bodies stacked up in homes, on porches, and in yards. The city opened six supplementary morgues to handle the volume, but even they were not enough. Families were forced to dig graves for their own dead when gravediggers refused to handle the terribly decomposed bodies. The dead and the dying were inescapable.

So were rumors, including the one that the sickness that gripped the city was not influenza but bubonic plague. The influenza caused cyanosis, or the bluish discoloration of the skin caused by the lack of oxygen, which resembled the Black Death's black spots, which were caused by bleeding under the skin.

In short supply, however, were doctors and nurses. Hundreds were serving in the military and, of those remaining—including medical students from the city's five medical schools—almost half of them would be sickened and hospitalized. The rest were fatigued and overwhelmed.

In one week in mid-October alone, Philadelphia lost 4,597 to influenza and influenza-related pneumonia.

AND ELSEWHERE

Chicago saw a mortality rate at Cook County Hospital of close to 40 percent and joined other cities in banning public gatherings, as well as coughing and sneezing without covering the nose and mouth with a handkerchief.

Everywhere, cities and towns came to a virtual standstill. People were afraid to leave their homes and went out of their way to avoid contact with others when they did. It was illegal in Prescott, Arizona, to shake hands. Frightened citizens wore surgical masks everywhere, watching helplessly as the disease crept across the country toward their towns.

In Atlanta, Georgia, the city council ordered all public gathering places closed for two months starting October 8; those who did not follow the order faced a $200 fine. Doctors were overwhelmed with hundreds of cases each, yet the city decided to allow the Southeastern Fair, a civic fair and parade, to go forward even as the rate of infection and the death toll rose. The authorities seemed determined to downplay the seriousness of the outbreak, underreporting death tolls and issuing reassuring statements even as the newspapers told a different story. On the last day of the Southeastern Fair, almost 3,500 new cases of influenza were reported in Georgia. That same day, Atlanta's leading public health official announced that the disease was "well under control."

Desperation was fueled by the severe shortage of medical assistance and the scarcity of any legitimate cure or treatment for influenza. People tried anything and everything to stay healthy or to get better. Some wore camphor or garlic around their neck to ward off the disease; others turned to patent medicines and disinfectants or heeded warnings to keep their feet dry.

In Alaska, the Inuit population was particularly hard hit. A relief expedition to Nome found that 176 of the city's 300 Inuit had died; smaller villages were wiped out or saw only a 15 percent survival rate. Entire families were killed. In Labrador, a settlement of Inuit saw all but 4 of 100 people sick; by the end of November, one-quarter of the population had died, and there was little for rescuers to do but bury the dead.

Canadians were also impacted by the disease, with 500,000 coming down with influenza in Quebec and 300,000 in

Joyful revelers celebrate Armistice Day in New York City. Despite warnings against public gatherings, the signing of the armistice treaty to mark the end of World War I gave people cause to rush out into the streets, most likely helping spread the virus to many more victims.

Ontario. Almost 23,000 of those died, 201 in Montreal on October 21 alone, creating such a shortage of hearses that coffins had to be transported by streetcar. People sickened and died in a matter of hours. A young woman in Toronto went to bed with no symptoms and was found dead the next morning by her roommate. In Labrador, one-third of the population died. In the town of Olak, 114 out of 266 people died. Dogs had to be shot by the hundreds to stop them from feeding on their late masters who had grown too weak to feed them and then died.

For October 1918, the death toll for the United States was 195,000, many from pneumonia caused by secondary bacterial infections. This variation of the flu also caused a primary viral pneumonia so virulent it led to extensive hemorrhaging, or bleeding, of the lungs. Many died in agony, some bleeding from their eyes, ears, and nose.

During this horror came cause for celebration as, on November 11, 1918, at 11 P.M. (on the eleventh hour of the eleventh day of the eleventh month), World War I, the cause of the massive mobilization of men from around the country that initially spread the disease, came to an end. In San Francisco, 300,000 people gathered to celebrate the end of the conflict, most of them wearing face masks to protect against infection.

By the end of November, the worst of the outbreak seemed to have passed. The inevitability of numbers was catching up with the deadly little virus. The official U.S. estimate put fatalities at 1 out of every 27 infected, an average that was spread across geographic areas with a variation in the severity of the outbreak. In the United States, the disease had hit first and hardest in the East and South, and less severely on the West Coast, while the middle of the country took the comparatively lightest hit.

But a pattern was emerging as to the way the influenza-virus plowed through the population. The number of susceptible victims decreased as the number of infected victims increased. Soon enough, the virus would run out of new victims to infect and, as those already infected were rendered immune to reinfection, it would have no new hosts in which to replicate and spread.

Soon, the deadly virus would reach a near-maximum efficiency, leaving it nowhere to go but into extinction.

Or mutation.

A PATTERN OF INFECTION

In the span of just 10 days in mid-October, Philadelphia went from a state of emergency with a week of 4,597 deaths to the lifting of the order closing public places. By November 11, influenza seemed to have been vanquished along with the foes in the just-ended European war. No new cases of influenza were reported that day.

The influenzavirus was running out of people to infect. And, because its genetic information is carried in its RNA rather than the more stable DNA, the virus continued its rapid mutation as it went through the population. Statistically, a mutated virus is likely to be less deadly than its predecessor and more like the majority of less lethal viruses.

The cycle of infection, the local epidemics that made up the global pandemic, was from six to eight weeks in cities and towns. In the more crowded army and naval bases, it was three to four weeks. After that, the virus ran out of victims, became less lethal, and then faded away.

In the first bases struck by influenza, 20 percent of infected soldiers developed pneumonia, 37 percent of whom died. That rate increased as it spread from camp to camp, with more than two-thirds of influenza patients developing pneumonia, 61 percent of whom died.

By the end of the cycle, only 7 percent of those infected on military bases were coming down with pneumonia, of whom about 18 percent died.

Infections in cities followed the same pattern across their own six- to eight-week cycles. In Boston, Baltimore, New York, New Orleans, and other cities hit early in the outbreak, victims suffered worse symptoms and higher fatalities than places that came at the end of it. San Antonio, Texas, was hit later in the cycle, suffering among the highest rate of infection—53.5 percent of the population, with at least one person in 98 percent of all households coming down with influenza—and the smallest rate of fatalities, under 1 percent.

As it ran its course through the population, the Spanish influenzavirus had mutated into a milder, less deadly form.

But that, too, was another part of the pattern of infection.

The second wave of the outbreak was at an end. But, just as the first wave had surged through Haskell County, Camp

Funston, and then spread outward from Kansas the previous March and April before virtually disappearing by June, this strain was not finished yet with the exhausted, depleted citizens of the United States. In the case of the influenza pandemic, bad news really did come in threes. The virus was still out there, staying alive in small pockets of infection and continuing to mutate, here and around the world.

5 The World

From Haskell County to Camp Funston to Boston and New York and then, by ship and by the tens of thousands, influenza spread across the world. Epidemiologists have since searched the public record for outbreaks of influenza predating the Kansas outbreak but have been unable to find any.

The spread started with the military population and moved like wildfire. Camps and bases across the United States were overwhelmed by disease. Preparations for war came to a standstill as all able-bodied men were pressed into service caring for the tens of thousands of sick.

But the movement of troops could not be slowed, and ships still departed regularly from ports in New York, Boston, Virginia, and up and down the Atlantic Coast, sending infected and sickened men across the sea to France.

And from there, troops joined other units in the filthy, rugged conditions experienced by those fighting at the front and in support units across Europe. It was a vicious cycle: A disease that should have remained a local outbreak in an isolated Kansas county was spread because of the war, which in turn created ideal conditions for the flu's further spread. The flu continued to change and adapt, honing its ability to replicate and spread in humans with greater efficiency. This was the Darwinian principle of "survival of the fittest" playing out at superspeed in comparison to the thousands of years of genetic adaptation on the human scale.

WESTERN EUROPE

The main destination for European-bound U.S. troops was France, and the first report of influenza was in early April 1918, at the port city of Brest, where 40 percent of American troops would arrive. Like the earliest cases in Kansas, the beginning of the first wave in Europe was relatively mild. Though fatalities were higher than usual for the flu, they were not so great as to raise any alarms.

But the disease was spreading quickly, from newly arrived Americans to a French naval command in Brest to a base near Chaumont where most of the 172 U.S. Marines stationed there were sickened; they all recovered.

Then, on April 10, the disease spread to a French army base; by the end of the month, it was in Paris.

In mid-April, the disease hit the British army like well-aimed German artillery. Hospital admissions in May 1918 among the British First Army numbered 36,473, with tens of thousands of less serious cases reporting sick. The Second Army was hit in late May; the Third Army right after it, cutting troop strengths by one-third. Troops returning to England soon brought the disease home with them.

The Germans were not spared the crippling effects of the disease, coming as it did at the start of the offensive that would prove to be Germany's last chance to win the war, in late April. The German forces were on the threshold of the last phase of a great push against the Allied armies when, suddenly, their armies stalled. The German commander

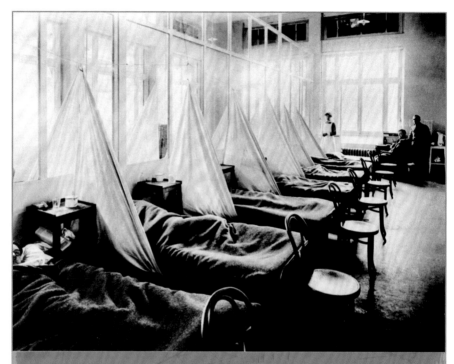

Because American troops sent to Europe were mainly stationed in France before being deployed to various locations in the war, influenza spread quickly among the ranks. Those soldiers who did not die as a result of the virus brought it back to the United States, where it continued to spread across the country. More people died as a result of the pandemic than from World War I.

blamed the delay on the influenza epidemic, which slashed his troop strength.

Unlike British, French, and German newspapers, whose government censors stopped them from printing news of the outbreaks to help maintain wartime morale, the Spanish press reported on the disease. The topic hit close to home as the king, Alphonse XIII, took ill with influenza. Because of Spaniards' leadership in reporting on the outbreak, this strain became known as the Spanish influenza.

As the influenzavirus surged across the continent, it underwent another mutation, and June and July saw record fatalities across England, Scotland, and Wales, while Germany erupted with a full-blown epidemic in June. Denmark and Norway followed in July; Holland and Sweden in August.

Deaths aboard transports between the United States and France reached alarming rates, one ship's log recording one or two deaths at 10- or 15-minute intervals all through the night. Bodies were buried at sea, but the sickness traveled in the living, many who might not yet show symptoms but who would remain contagious until long after the ship had docked and they were separated into units across the continent.

The death rate aboard ships was so high, President Woodrow Wilson considered stopping the shipment of men to Europe until the epidemic could be brought under control. His commander of the army, General Peyton March, convinced the president that every precaution was being taken to weed out the sick, and the uninterrupted flow of men to Europe was vital in the effort to keep the pressure on a German government that was on the verge of surrender.

Even if those transports had been stopped, the influenzavirus had already taken hold in Europe. The late-October Allied offensive at Meuse-Argonne was slowed by the high number of sick. For the Americans and French, influenza was the cause of most medical evacuations.

SPREAD AND MAXIMUM EFFICIENCY

Influenza hit India around May 29, carried to Bombay aboard a transport ship. First those around the docks fell ill, then the flu spread through the rest of the country, following the railroad lines from the coast to the vast interior.

Also at the end of May, the disease hit Shanghai, China, eventually sickening half the population of Chungking. When it spread to New Zealand and Australia, 30 percent of Sydney was taken ill. Australia quickly imposed a strict quarantine that kept the worst of the later, more deadly waves out of the country and, as a result, suffered the lowest fatality rate of any industrialized Western nation.

Still, as was the case with the initial wave of the disease in the United States, this first pass through Europe and the East produced a relatively small increase in influenza and influenza-related death. One U.S. base saw only one death out of 613 hospital admissions; only 4 out of 10,313 sick British

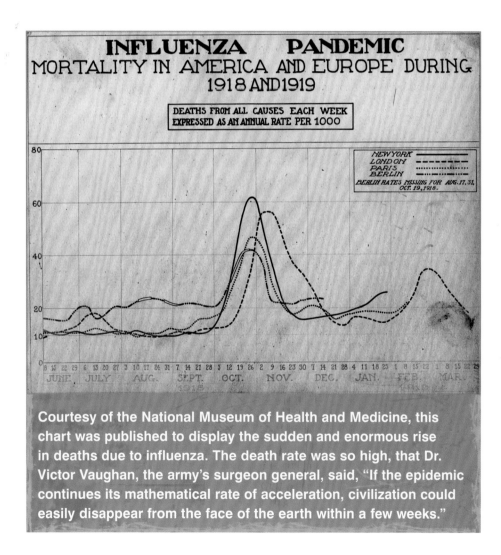

INFLUENZA PANDEMIC
MORTALITY IN AMERICA AND EUROPE DURING 1918 AND 1919

DEATHS FROM ALL CAUSES EACH WEEK EXPRESSED AS AN ANNUAL RATE PER 1000

Courtesy of the National Museum of Health and Medicine, this chart was published to display the sudden and enormous rise in deaths due to influenza. The death rate was so high, that Dr. Victor Vaughan, the army's surgeon general, said, "If the epidemic continues its mathematical rate of acceleration, civilization could easily disappear from the face of the earth within a few weeks."

Worldwide Deaths from Influenza

Without more accurate records, the true extent of the devastation of the 1918–1919 influenza pandemic will never be known, but with a worldwide death toll in the tens of millions or more, its effect on the world was enormous. And the lessons it has to teach for a future pandemic are priceless.

In the United States, fewer than half the states kept records accurate enough to be included in a database of diseases kept by the U.S. Public Health Service. In the undeveloped world, which included India, South America, Africa, China, and large portions of Russia, then in the middle of a civil war, recordkeeping was not just poor, it was nonexistent. In 1927, an American Medical Association study put the pandemic's worldwide death toll at 21 million, but every study since has steadily revised the total upward.

A 1940 study placed the final number of dead at 40 million to 100 million, but even those figures may be conservative considering what is not known of the total number of dead in such densely populated but poorly reported countries as India, the Soviet Union, and China.

The world's population in 1918 was 1.8 billion, making those 100 million deaths a staggering 5 percent of the people in the world. A similar death toll today, with the world's population at approximately 6.8 billion, would result in almost 350 million dead.

The United States lost roughly 0.65 percent of its population to influenza; Italy, approximately 1 percent. Mexico lost between 5 and 9 percent of its young adults to the disease, 4 percent of its total population.

sailors. The virus was still gaining a foothold in the population, forging its own lineage of mutation toward its maximum efficiency as a man-killer.

During the second week of July, London saw 287 influenza-related deaths; Birmingham, England, 126. American troops continued arriving in Brest by the boatload, more than three-quarters of a million men by war's end, mingling with the men of different armies and nations. Influenza also reached West Africa by ship, infecting local laborers, who then took the infection home to their families and neighbors. By August 27, 500 of 600 laborers at a port in Sierra Leone were too ill to work. A transport from New Zealand taking on coal at Freetown came down with 900 cases of influenza three weeks later. The official estimate in Sierra Leone was that three percent of the African population died from influenza-related causes.

Then, as elsewhere, the rate of new infections began to lessen in severity and intensity. Death rates dropped, and finally, the disease just seemed to disappear as if there was no one left who could possibly be made sick.

The virus was particularly lethal in areas of poverty and poor sanitation. Ten percent of the entire population of the Mexican state of Chiapas died; Cape Town was typical of South African cities and towns, losing four percent of the African population to the disease within four weeks. Entire villages in Gambia were wiped out by influenza, while Buenos Aires, Argentina, saw 55 percent of its population taken ill; in Brazil, the attack rate was 33 percent.

One-third of the Japanese population became ill, 10 percent of the population of Guam died, and 7 percent of both Russia's and Iran's population died.

In Fiji, 14 percent of the population died in just 16 days. Western Samoa lost 22 percent of its 38,302 people to the disease, brought to the island by a steamer.

India was hit harder than most, the influenza striking twice as fast as an epidemic of bubonic plague that had swept through the nation in 1900. The disease did not discriminate: 10 percent of natives taken ill soon died, and 9 percent of European troops died as well. Deaths for Indian troops were even higher, with more than 21 percent eventually dying.

In Bombay, almost 1,500 people died during one week in mid-July. The disease took months to pulse through the Indian subcontinent. Mail deliveries were suspended, courts closed, and industry ground to a halt because 60 percent of the laborers were too ill to work.

Many areas of India were already suffering from crop failures due to a dry rainy season, but even the reduced crops could not be fully harvested because there, too, the workers, those 20 to 40 years old, were afflicted by the disease. As a result, food production fell by 20 percent, and prices doubled, driving the poor into the crowded cities which helped spread the influenzavirus.

So many people were dying in the Punjab region that survivors quickly ran out of firewood with which to build the traditional funeral pyres to burn the bodies. It is estimated that as many as 20 million people died on the Indian subcontinent alone, a staggering number that made the death toll on the European battlefields pale in comparison.

THE THIRD WAVE

On October 7, 1918, the U.S. troop ship *Leviathan* docked at Brest. Even before the ship had set sail from New York with troops from Vermont, via a camp in New Jersey, 120 troops had to be taken off the ship because they were sick. Eleven thousand men in total traveled aboard the big, jammed ship. Two thousand men at a time took ill during the voyage; dozens died and were buried at sea.

Thirty-one men died the day the ship docked in France. More than 1,000 were too ill to leave the ship. The rest, many of them also ill, had to march four miles (6.4 km) through a cold rain to their barracks. Four died on the march, and in the days that followed, the troops from Vermont alone lost almost 200 men.

Between September 1 and the end of fighting on November 11, 1918, American army losses in battle totaled more than 35,000 men, while influenza and pneumonia claimed almost that many during the six months until April 1919. The navy lost more men to influenza in the last quarter of 1918 than they had to the Germans during the entire year.

During October 1918, the commander of the American forces in Europe urgently cabled Washington for additional medical personnel and hospital units. He had more than 45,000 men hospitalized, and 10 percent of them were dying from pneumonia and other complications. And those numbers did not include the endless turnover of wounded from the battlefield. Any and all medical facilities were overwhelmed to the point where they were little more than holding areas for the sick and dying.

By late November, the second wave had made its way around the world, inflicting a horrible toll. In Paris, 50 percent of all patients who developed influenza-related complications died. In Frankfurt, Germany, 27 percent of those hospitalized died.

But then, as suddenly as it had arrived, influenza disappeared, and relieved people the world over started to return to their normal lives. Orders banning public gatherings, closing schools and churches, and enforcing the wearing of face masks were canceled.

And then, only a few weeks later, the virus, having undergone another mutation, struck again.

The change in the virus was not radical. In fact, the shift was small enough that those who had been sickened in the second wave were likely to be immune from this new variation, but it was significant enough that it set the epidemic in motion again.

A former German passenger ship, *Leviathan* was remodeled for the American military and became the largest ship in the U.S. Navy and the world. Used for troop transport, the ship's close quarters proved dangerous, as many of its military personnel fell ill on the way to France.

In January and February, it struck anew in Australia—albeit as a strain far weaker and less lethal than any other in the world—and elsewhere. In Paris, the death toll in February 1919 was 2,676, with 1,517 more following in March.

It made its way through Britain, Italy, and elsewhere and then came back to the United States with returning troops. In Washington, D.C., President Woodrow Wilson's wife and members of his staff became ill in late March 1919. A few days later, in Versailles, France, to negotiate the terms of the peace, the president also became seriously ill and was bedridden for four days.

In New York City, it was estimated that 21,000 children had been orphaned, while tiny Berlin, New Hampshire, was left with 24 orphans. The death toll in New York and Chicago for February and March 1919 was 11,000.

Reliable statistics for the deaths in many parts of the world such as India, rural Russia, China, Africa, and South America were never kept. Even in developed nations, public officials were too overwhelmed helping the sick to keep reliable counts of victims, and many died without ever seeing a physician.

6 Combating the Pandemic

While millions suffered and died, the medical community was not sitting by idle. Since the war had been a threat looming on the horizon, several of the leading medical and epidemiological minds of the time had been waving red flags of warning about contagious disease. Most of the military's public health efforts were focused on preventing STDs (sexually transmitted diseases), but such noted physicians as Army Surgeon General William Gorgas and Johns Hopkins University's Dr. William Henry Welch were dogged in their efforts to not let the problem get lost in the chaos of war.

Dr. Gorgas predicted this simple formula for disaster: One virulent strain of a disease plus the unprecedented mix of people from across the country, added to overcrowded and often questionable sanitary conditions and multiplied by international troop movements, equals pandemic.

There was nothing anyone in the medical establishment of the time could do to stop outbreaks, but if proper attention was paid to sanitation, heating, clothing, nutrition, and space requirements for soldiers and sailors, diseases could, perhaps, be contained and controlled.

But this was wartime, and money, time, and resources were scarce, so soldiers were processed through training as quickly as possible, as many at a time as possible. These were healthy young men, training for hardship and conditions worse than what they were experiencing at the crowded camps. The government was accustomed, reluctantly but by historic precedent, to accepting a certain amount of troop loss to disease.

MODERN MEDICINE

Medical science had made great leaps in its understanding, combating, and, in some cases, prevention of disease in the 50 years before the war. Advances in public sanitation and personal hygiene had been major and significant, as had been progress in identifying and even, in some cases, creating vaccines against diseases. For those attempting to create drugs that would not only prevent disease but also actively fight it in those already infected, inspiration was to be found in the work of Dr. Paul Ehrlich (1854–1915), the German research physician who in 1909, along with his student Sukehachiro Hata, discovered Salvarsan, a treatment for syphilis. Salvarsan was the first antibiotic drug in modern medicine.

From Dr. Ehrlich's work came research that would lead, in the decades to come, to additional treatments for bacterial infection, including sulfa drugs, penicillin, and other antibiotics. Science had known since the end of the eighteenth century that a dead or weakened sample of an infectious agent introduced into a previously uninfected person—through inoculation with infected blood, saliva, or pus—can give immunity to that disease. Vaccines already prevented a variety of livestock disease, including hog cholera and anthrax. Smallpox could now be immunized against, as could yellow fever, typhoid, cholera, and plague.

Antitoxins, or agents capable of counteracting the toxins that cause various diseases or adverse reactions, were available for diphtheria, meningitis, gangrene, snakebites, dysentery, and tetanus (a bacterial infection also known as lockjaw that

Many officials were reluctant to declare pandemic status for their cities, which led to misinformation and a false sense of security. During a baseball game, players and an umpire wear masks to prevent infection *(above)*, but events like this were later banned in many places across the United States to stop public gatherings from encouraging the spread of the virus.

causes painful, rigid muscle contractions, especially in the neck and jaw), and, in fact, General Gorgas had ordered such vaccines and antitoxins to be stockpiled for emergency use. Many new army doctors were being trained at the Rockefeller Institute, an international health organization sponsored by oil magnate John D. Rockefeller and home to some of the best medical minds in the world.

The Rockefeller Institute was a leading medical research facility. Its scientists had been working on a vaccine for influenza, but they faced the same problem as everyone else in the field: How do you create a vaccine containing the influenzavirus to stimulate the body's immune system when the virus will have mutated by the time the vaccine could be put into production? Developing a cure for diphtheria or tetanus, diseases that were stable and unchanging, was challenging enough. Aiming at a moving target such as the constantly mutating influenzavirus was beyond the science of the time.

But in June 1918, despite the outbreaks in Kansas and elsewhere, influenza was the least of Gorgas's worries. He was concerned about measles, which was then affecting various places around the globe and could, in pandemic form, lead to a high death toll. By 1917, doctors at the Rockefeller Institute had made progress in a serum for curing two of the three types of pneumonia, which would be the primary cause of death for most influenza victims. Twelve thousand troops on Long Island received the Rockefeller vaccine. The 19,000 troops who did not receive the vaccine served as the control, or sample group. Three months later, not one of the vaccinated soldiers developed pneumonia, while there were 101 cases in the control group.

PNEUMONIA

The pneumonia that struck victims of influenza was of a tougher strain than researchers were accustomed to seeing. The three main types of pneumonia were: lobar pneumonia, which infects a single lobe, or section, of a lung; multilobar, which infects more than one lobe; and interstitial, involving the areas between the alveoli, which are spherical structures on the lungs that are responsible for exchanging gases with the blood.

In healthy lungs, the tissue is pink and spongy, transmitting the oxygen we inhale to the blood, which then circulates it through the body. When the lungs are invaded by the bacterial or viral agents that cause the different types of pneumonia, all the cells and fluids involved in an active immune system invade as well. The infected alveoli become clogged with dead cells, antibodies, proteins, and enzymes that prevent them from transmitting oxygen to the blood.

When lungs do not function properly, the body begins to fail. Lack of oxygen first causes cyanosis, leading to damage to the body's other organs before they shut down and die.

But this pneumonia showed few signs of the sorts of damage usually associated with the bacterial, multilobar pneumonias. The invading flu virus was so powerful that it destroyed lung tissue on its own, usually in a matter of hours or days. Lungs were so filled with blood and debris that they remained inflated even when removed from the deceased. These fragile balloons, so essential to life, were being shredded by the disease. Pathologists had never seen this sort of damage before.

Doctors knew that the pneumonia, however severe, was a secondary symptom of the influenza. They understood that to stop the spread of the killer pneumonia, the influenza would first need to be brought under control. This could be done by rigorous containment and quarantine methods, both impossible because of the war, or by medical means.

They also thought that influenza was caused by a bacterium—*Bacillus influenzae*—named by Dr. Richard Pfeiffer (1858–1945), the man who discovered it. Dr. Pfeiffer's reputation for his work with cholera and typhoid, as well as the knowledge that diseases such as anthrax, plague, and cholera were caused by bacteria, lead the scientific community to accept his conclusions without question.

Doctors looked for signs of *Bacillus influenzae* in their patients during the 1918 outbreak in order to confirm the diagnosis of influenza and to attempt to develop an antitoxin to cure the disease or a vaccine to prevent it.

In addition to the mystery surrounding the destruction of the lungs by the disease, many doctors were surprised to find no evidence of *Bacillus influenzae* in most of their patients. Researchers at the Rockefeller Institute conducted experiments that suggested the cause of the outbreak was not bacterial after all.

THE HUNT FOR A PATHOGEN

Researchers the world over quickly turned their attention to influenza and pneumonia. Work at the Rockefeller Institute and at the New York City Department of Public Health in particular would prove significant.

Samples of sputum, urine, and blood were taken from living patients and the dead to be prepared for study and examination, but no sign of *Bacillus influenzae* was found, although the fault for that was believed to be the difficulty in isolating and growing this particular bacteria.

Finally, a researcher in the New York laboratory did isolate the bacillus with results that seemed to be conclusive, but which did not prevent Dr. William H. Park (1863–1939), the head of the lab, from wiring a colleague that "There is of course the possibility that some unknown filterable virus (a virus small enough to pass through a fine-pored filter) may be the starting point."

In fact, further research showed that the bacillus was deadly, but the symptoms in animal testing did not resemble those of influenza and human testing was too slow and proving likewise inconclusive.

In Philadelphia, Dr. Paul Lewis of the Philips Institute recognized that animal testing for the disease was useless. The only animal on Earth affected by this strain of influenza was man, therefore the only accurate test for it was human testing. He also theorized that using the blood of infected horses to extract a serum, as was the procedure for other vaccines and serums, would be ineffectual.

Instead, Dr. Lewis drew the blood of volunteers who had survived the disease and created a serum that he hoped would

Dr. Robert Koch, pictured here with his wife, won the Nobel Peace Prize in 1905 for his exceptional accomplishments in studying and limiting the spread of anthrax, typhus, tuberculosis, and other deadly diseases. Considered to be one of the founding fathers of modern bacteriology, Koch discovered the bacteria that caused tuberculosis.

transfer the survivors' influenza antibodies to the recipient and produce an immunity. Though not a scientifically controlled experiment, this approach seemed to produce encouraging results, with only 1 death out of the 36 pneumonia patients who received the serum.

Still, concrete proof of the true cause of the epidemic eluded scientists. Dr. Lewis had found *Bacillus influenzae* in living patients and the dead, but he was also finding a pneumococcus and a hemolytic streptococcus, both bacteria also associated with pneumonia. Dr. Lewis was looking for a fast solution, a serum that might cure the disease and stop its rapid spread, so he prepared a vaccine using cultures of all the pathogens they

The Germ Theory of Disease

In 1876, the German doctor Robert Koch (1843–1910) became the first scientist to link the cause of a disease directly to a specific bacteria, proving that anthrax, a disease common to cattle, sheep, horses, and goats, and which proved fatal when transmitted to humans, was caused by anthrax bacilli, which had been discovered in 1850 by Pierre-Francoise Olive Rayer and Casimir-Joseph Davaine.

Dr. Koch harvested anthrax bacilli from the spleens of diseased farm animals and inoculated mice with the bacteria, which caused the mice to contract the disease, confirming that it could be transmitted by blood. He also grew a pure strain of anthrax in a sterile medium that, when injected into other animals, gave them the disease, proving conclusively that it was the bacillus and not anything else in the blood of the infected animals that caused the disease.

He also gave the research world Koch's Postulates, the rules by which an organism is proved to be the cause of a disease or lesion:

1. The specific organism should be shown to be present in all cases of animals suffering from a specific disease but should not be found in healthy animals.
2. The specific microorganism should be isolated from the diseased animal and grown in pure culture on artificial laboratory media.
3. This freshly isolated microorganism, when inoculated into a healthy laboratory animal, should cause the same disease seen in the original animal.
4. The microorganism should be reisolated in pure culture from the experimental infection.

had isolated from patients. Into it went types I and II of *Bacillus influenzae*, pneumococcus, and hemolytic streptococcus.

Sixty people received the first batch of serum, resulting in only 3 infections and no deaths, compared to a control group that saw 10 cases of pneumonia and 3 deaths.

Meanwhile, at the Rockefeller Institute, Dr. Oswald Avery (1877–1955) remained skeptical of *Bacillus influenzae* as the culprit. At first, he found no sign of bacterial invasion in the lungs of victims, then, like Dr. Lewis, he found it. Some reports from around the country confirmed his finding; others did not. If the bacillus was the cause, it was proving awfully elusive. He needed to find a foolproof way to grow bacilli. This he did, step by step, over several weeks, and his methods would allow anyone to grow the bacilli if they were present in the sample.

TREATING THE SICK

Doctors everywhere were unveiling vaccines by mid-October. The work of Dr. William H. Park and Dr. Paul Lewis was distributed, while the army shipped 2 million doses of its own vaccine, developed at the Army Medical School in Washington, for its soldiers and civilian employees.

Short of discovering a cure, all most doctors could do was try and make their patients as comfortable as possible. Sometimes aspirin and morphine were the best they could offer, or maybe codeine to alleviate a severe cough. Oxygen could be administered to help with congested lungs. Stimulants could also be administered to boost the heart rate and give patients the strength to fight the disease.

Others tried less conventional treatments, many out of desperation in the face of overwhelming odds. In Philadelphia, one doctor wrote to the *Journal of the American Medical Association* (*JAMA*) about his idea to raise the body's alkaline levels to render it "poor soil for bacterial growth." Another injected hydrogen peroxide into the blood of 25 patients,

With no cure for the deadly virus that was wiping out populations around the world, people turned to folk remedies, like the boys seen here wearing bags of camphor around their necks. Other remedies attempted by desperate citizens included tying red ribbons around their right arms and ingesting lumps of sugar flavored with kerosene.

resulting in 13 recoveries and 12 deaths. Still others tried every sort of vaccine on influenza and pneumonia patients, reasoning that even though they had been created to fight different diseases, they still *might* boost the immune system or even fight the infection.

Another letter to *JAMA* came from a doctor who thought to prevent influenza by using irritating chemicals to stimulate the flow of mucus, thereby preventing the pathogen from being able to attach to the body long enough to multiply and gain a foothold.

In Europe, physicians tried any number of serums and chemical curatives, including arsenic, chemical dyes, mercuric chloride, and metallic solutions. Enemas of warm milk and a disinfectant were recommended. Some doctors even went back to bleeding as a cure, while others advocated a treatment called cupping, which used a flame in a glass container placed on the skin—the flame burned off the oxygen inside the container to create a vacuum that, in theory, drew poisons from the body.

Home remedies, such as necklaces of camphor balls or garlic, were tried. Mustard plasters were applied to patients, raising blisters that were then drained of pus, which was mixed with morphine and other ingredients and then injected back into the patient. Patent medicines—fraudulent medications that were usually little more than mixtures of alcohol, flavoring, and whatever ingredients, good or bad, the producer happened to have on hand—were on sale everywhere as surefire cures. Cotton face masks were produced by the millions, and some people would only go out in public wearing a gas mask.

"HUMILIATING BUT TRUE"

In the end, there was little science could do to combat the pandemic. And that remains true to this day. While vaccines do offer the public a measure of protection against the outbreak of a predicted strain, we have seen that all that is required for the unpredictable is a routine mutation of a single virus.

But scientists have kept studying the problem, with *Bacillus influenzae* still being bounced back and forth as the cause of influenza. Often it would be found where it did not belong, and just as often, it would be absent from places it should have been present.

Observing the national and international frenzy to investigate the pandemic and find a cure or a vaccine, Dr. Welch predicted: "I think that this epidemic is likely to pass away, and we are no more familiar with the control of the disease than we were in the epidemic of 1889. It is humiliating, but true."

In the end, all anybody could really do was wait for the dying to end.

7 Aftermath

On February 7, 1920, influenza struck again, a last surge that would end the pandemic not with a whimper but with a bang. Over the next two months, the disease again ravaged most of the world. New York City had more cases reported in a single day during this final outbreak than during the three waves of 1918–1919.

And long after the last case of influenza in the pandemic had been diagnosed and recovered, its effects were still being felt, both economically and physically. The Red Cross reported that death had not been influenza's only gift; it left in its wake ". . . a trail of lowered vitality . . . nervous breakdown and other [symptoms] which now threaten thousands of people. It left widows and orphans and dependent old people. It has reduced many of these families to poverty and acute distress. The havoc is wide spread, reaching all parts of the United States and all classes of people."

People everywhere complained of lowered energy and of not feeling right or like their old selves. More than two-thirds of the influenza victims examined by public health officials in Cincinnati, Ohio, were found to require additional medical treatment, while 643 of them suffered heart problems.

This strain of influenza affected almost every organ in the body and left behind damaged and ruined muscle and tissue as evidence of its presence. Pathologists found that virtually every case they examined showed at least some degree of kidney and adrenal gland damage, inflammation of the pericardium (the sac that protects the heart), bleeding in the brain, and muscle degeneration. In addition, rib cages were torn apart by the disease's toxic effects and by the stresses of coughing, and lungs were often so badly shredded that an army doctor could only compare them to those damaged from the poison gases used in warfare.

THE SCIENTIFIC COMMUNITY

Yet for all the horrors wrought by the pandemic, some good did begin to emerge in the form of advances in public health monitoring and services. As early as October 30, 1918, the New York City municipal health department organized an influenza commission of leading scientists. City health commissioner Dr. Biggs was angry, opening the conference with an admonition that they had seen this epidemic coming long before it exploded but had taken no action and made no preparations.

The conference had trouble agreeing whether this had even been an outbreak of influenza at all. Because so little was known about the disease and because symptoms often included cyanosis and bleeding from lungs ravaged by the powerful influenzavirus, some argued that perhaps what they were dealing with was instead the plague.

And, once again, *Bacillus influenzae*'s guilt as the influenza pathogen was called into question. It was found in 30 percent of healthy people examined by the Rockefeller Institute and was absent in some people suffering from influenza. Could it instead be an as-yet-undetected virus causing the disease? Researchers were looking into the question.

The conference did agree to continue researching the disease in the laboratory as well as by conducting epidemiological investigations, tracing the course of the infection through communities, taking detailed personal histories of the sickened and healthy alike, and seeking connections between influenza and other diseases as well as factors such as diet.

A month after the New York conference, the American Public Health Association, funded by a life insurance company, created a Committee on Statistical Study of the Influenza Epidemic to show how public health statistics could be used to predict and prevent future epidemics. Two months later, the U.S. Census Bureau, the navy and army surgeon generals, and the Public Health Service began a statistical office to track influenza and other infectious diseases.

IN THE LABORATORY

In early 1919, Dr. Park, chief of the laboratory division of the New York City Health Department, and his deputy, Dr. Anna Williams (1863–1954), were finally able to put the mystery of *Bacillus influenzae* to rest. They proved that while the bacillus was often present in influenza victims, so were dozens of other bacteria, and that, like pneumococcus, which is responsible for pneumonia, there seemed to be dozens of strains of *Bacillus influenzae*—each different enough from the others to make a serum effective against them all impossible.

The doctors reported that: "evidence of multiple strains seems to be absolutely against the influenza bacillus being the cause of the pandemic. It appears to us impossible that we should miss the epidemic strain in so many cases while obtaining some other strain so abundantly. The influenza bacilli, like the streptococci and pneumococci, are in all probability merely very important secondary invaders." Echoing a thought earlier put in a telegram to a colleague by Dr. Park,

Dr. Williams noted in her diary that "evidence points to a filterable virus being the cause."

BUT WHERE WAS THIS VIRUS?

The answer to that would need to wait for more than a decade, but the exhaustive research into the disease would, in the meantime, lead to numerous discoveries beneficial to science and the world.

(continues on page 88)

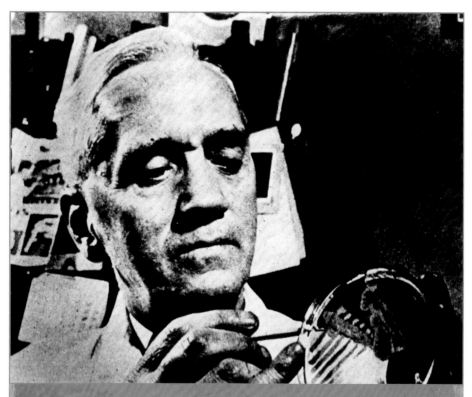

Sir Alexander Fleming *(above)* accidentally discovered penicillin when he noticed a fungus's antibacterial properties. After the development of penicillin, Fleming warned the public not to over-prescribe the antibiotic, a practice that could lead to bacteria developing immunity to the drug.

Other Epidemic Diseases

HIV/AIDS was virtually unknown before the early 1980s, yet by 2002, according to the National Center for HIV, STD and TB Prevention at the Centers for Disease Control and Prevention (CDC), there were almost 900,000 cases of AIDS, with close to 500,000 deaths in the United States alone. By 1981, 422 cases had been diagnosed in the United States, with 159 deaths. In 1982, the disease was named, and in 1983, researchers at the Pasteur Institute in Paris discovered the AIDS virus. By 2003, more than 40 million people worldwide were infected with HIV/AIDS; in that year alone, 5 million new cases were diagnosed, and there were 3 million deaths.

Bovine spongiform encephalopathy (BSE), or "mad cow disease," was first reported in the cattle population of Great Britain in 1986. By 1993, there were almost 1,000 new cases a month. BSE is a fatal brain disorder caused by an unknown pathogen that destroys cows' brain cells, ultimately forming spongelike holes in their brain. In the 1990s, several people in Britain died of a variant of a rare brain disorder similar to BSE called Creutzfeldt-Jakob disease (CJD). The variant seemed to have been contracted from eating the meat of an infected cow. BSE has since been reported in more than 30 countries in Europe, the Middle East, and the Far East. To protect itself from an outbreak of BSE, the United States imposed restrictions on the importation of at-risk livestock and their products, including meat, bonemeal, and glands, from countries where BSE had been reported, including Canada. Despite these precautions, a case of mad cow disease was reported in the United States in December 2003, forcing other nations, including Japan, the largest importer of American beef, to impose their own bans on the importation and sale of U.S. beef products.

In 2003, the world was gripped by an outbreak of SARS, or severe acute respiratory syndrome, a disease that was unknown in March of that year but which had by mid-April reached at least 18 countries, infecting more than 2,000 people and killing nearly 100 victims (a death rate of 4.9 percent, compared to the 5 percent death rate of the flu epidemic of 1918).

While a healthy person usually recovered from the cold-like SARS virus, which caused chills, headache, fever, muscle soreness, and a severe cough, it quickly proved fatal to the very young, the very old, and to people with weakened immune systems.

By the end of April, less than seven weeks after SARS had been documented, contagious disease specialists at the World Health Organization (WHO) and the CDC had identified and named the virus responsible, identified the pathogen, and mapped its genetic structure. By contrast, it took more than four years of investigation, from roughly 1979 to 1982, to identify the virus responsible for HIV. SARS is, according to the CDC, a previously unrecognized coronavirus, a relative of the virus that causes the common cold. By sharing information about the SARS virus, the world's health organizations were able to keep a potential epidemic from erupting. By May, approximately 5,000 cases in 27 countries had caused almost 300 deaths, and while those numbers would rise, the outbreak began to subside by the end of the year thanks to stringent public health efforts.

(continued from page 85)

In his research into the cause of influenza, England's Dr. Alexander Fleming (1881–1955) focused on developing a medium in which to grow the bacillus. He settled upon a petri dish (a shallow dish used to culture, or grow, bacteria) to grow the bacteria staphylococcus. In 1928, he left just such a petri dish uncovered for two days. He later found an unfamiliar mold that had stopped the growth of the bacillus.

A substance extracted from the mold, which he called "penicillin," was responsible for inhibiting the growth of the staphylococcus, as well as a great many other bacteria, including diphtheria, pneumococcus, and goncococcus, but it had no effect on the influenza bacillus. Dr. Fleming put penicillin to work, not as an antibiotic, but to kill contaminating bacteria in his *Bacillus influenzae* cultures. More than a decade later, scientists funded by the Rockefeller Foundation developed Fleming's mold into the antibiotic wonder drug, penicillin.

The work of British scientist Fred Griffith (1879–1941) proved that certain types of pneumococcus change under certain conditions, from harmless to lethal in mice. The Rockefeller Institute's Dr. Avery was fascinated by this and spent the next decade seeking the transformative agent in the bacteria.

One by one, he went through every chemical component of the tiny bacteria—protein, lipids (fatty acids), carbohydrates—until all he had left were nucleic acids, leading him to deoxyribonucleic acids, or DNA. DNA had been discovered in the 1860s, but, as no one understood its function, it was ignored by geneticists who at the time, believed that genetic information was carried by more complex protein molecules.

With his demonstration in 1944 that the transformed pneumococcus passed changes in the DNA on to its offspring, Dr. Avery proved that these nucleic acids carried genetic code between the generations. In 1955, James Watson (born 1928) and Francis Crick (1916–2004) discovered the double-helix structure of DNA and unraveled the mystery of how this information was passed.

SWINE INFLUENZA

In a 1931 issue of the *Journal of Experimental Medicine*, Dr. Richard E. Shope of the Rockefeller Institute published three papers about influenza, including his discovery of the long-elusive cause of influenza in swine, found while studying an epidemic of swine influenza in Iowa.

And as had long been suspected but until then unproven, it was a virus.

Dr. Shope believed the Spanish influenzavirus had most likely developed in swine, where it underwent a mutation that rendered it relatively harmless to the animals but potentially

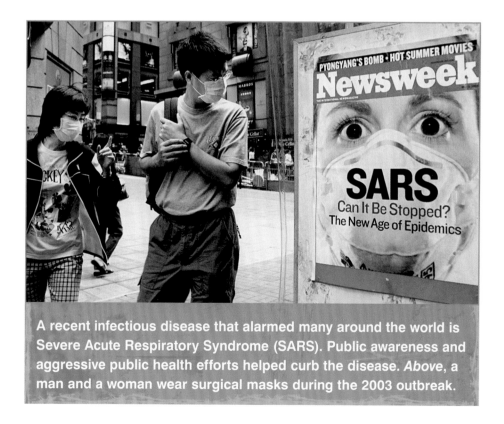

A recent infectious disease that alarmed many around the world is Severe Acute Respiratory Syndrome (SARS). Public awareness and aggressive public health efforts helped curb the disease. *Above*, a man and a woman wear surgical masks during the 2003 outbreak.

deadly to people. He also proved that it was possible to pass an influenza-like disease from one pig to another, and antibodies taken from human survivors of the 1918 pandemic were shown to grant the animals immunity from this strain of influenza.

In 1933, the human infectious agent was filtered from throat secretions of human influenza victims and used to infect ferrets with influenza. This agent was a virus similar to the one that caused the swine influenza. The influenza B virus was isolated in 1940 and the influenza C strain in 1950.

In 1941, a vaccine against influenza was developed using killed cultures, or dead viruses. These allowed the body to develop immunity to specific types of influenza without risk of infection. The impurities in many of these early vaccines could, however, cause headache, fever, and other severe side effects, but these were preferable to a new pandemic. No one was willing to risk another outbreak, certainly not while the country was again mobilized for war and on the move across the globe. The first doses of the vaccine went, for that reason, to military personnel.

Vaccination against influenza in the United States and the rest of the developed world has become routine. Every year, the vaccine's formula, the specific strains of influenza it will protect against, changes to reflect the particular strains the World Health Organization's Global Influenza Surveillance Network (established in 1952 as a network composed of four WHO Collaborating Centres and 112 institutions in 83 countries) believes will be dominant in the coming year.

Influenza, though still a threat, is at least no longer quite the scientific mystery.

THE 1918 INFLUENZAVIRUS DECONSTRUCTED

The 1918–1919 pandemic would have to wait until 2005 to reveal its ultimate secret. In 1999, efforts were undertaken to map the genome, or genetic sequence, of the virus. An article in the *Journal of General Virology* in 2003 explained how samples of the virus were obtained 81 years after the pandemic.

"Two of the (three) strains came from American soldiers who died on 26 September 1918: one in Camp Upton (New York, USA) and one in Fort Jackson (South Carolina, USA). The third came from an Inuit woman who died in mid-November 1918 in a remoter village on the Seward Peninsula of Alaska (USA)." Two other samples were from influenza victims who were treated but then died from pneumonia at the Royal London Hospital in the United Kingdom, one in November 1918 and the other in February 1919.

These samples, from victims ranging across six months and thousands of miles, showed that the virus remained remarkably stable, differing from one another by only two or three nucleotides, the basic building blocks of nucleic acids, or one percent of their genetic sequence.

The *Journal of General Virology* article casts doubt on the 1918 pandemic strain's origins in the bird population, noting that the genetic sequence is "related closely to ... the first influenza virus isolated from swine. The similarity suggests that the human pandemic influenza virus became established in swine, in which it changed very slowly."

The report also points out that "the 1918 pandemic sequence is related more closely to avian H1s than to any other mammalian H1s and has many avian features ... Since pigs can be infected with both avian and human strains, and various reassortants have been isolated from pigs, they have been proposed as an intermediary in the generation of reassortant pandemic strains." In other words, pigs are the perfect breeding ground for the reassortment, or antigen drift, of viruses that can affect mammals and birds.

A 2006 study by scientists at the University of Wisconsin–Madison, which was reported in the January 18, 2007,

Asian countries have stepped up efforts in testing animals and studying the avian flu virus in order to minimize the chances of a human outbreak. This particular strain of flu currently affects birds only, but there have been cases of pigs and cats infected with this virus. One reason for this could be the close contact animals have together, as seen here in this picture of chicks resting on pigs in Indonesia.

issue of *Nature*, revealed the deadliest mystery of the 1918–1919 pandemic—the cause of the devastating damage the disease did to the lungs.

Samples of the virus were recovered from victims of the pandemic and put through a genetic process that made the virus fully functional again. Laboratory monkeys were then infected, and they developed the same deadly respiratory ailment that shredded the lungs of so many of the pandemic victims.

This immunity response is similar to one seen most recently in the H5N1 strain of avian influenza, which, while it has claimed 150 lives in Asia, has not yet shown itself capable of spreading easily among humans. Researchers continue the search for the mechanism that allows the influenzavirus to spread so rapidly and with such virulence.

8 The Future

From the available evidence, most pandemics seem to have their origins in Asia, where, due to large populations living in close contact with birds and swine, the likelihood of a virus crossing over to humans is vastly increased.

Immediately following the pandemic, the American Medical Association sponsored a comprehensive international study conducted by the editor of the *Journal of Infectious Disease*. The study began in China, where, by the odds presented by history, the outbreak most likely originated. But influenza did not appear in China until June 1918, months after the Haskell County outbreak. The story was the same in every nation the study looked at; some had experienced local outbreaks, even epidemics, but nothing that matched the ferocity and virulence of the pandemic strain of the virus.

All the evidence pointed to the United States as the origin of the pandemic. The outbreaks in the spring of 1918 clearly showed the disease spreading through military bases and then jumping to neighboring civilian populations before boarding troop and merchant ships for Europe.

Later studies in Britain and Australia agreed. The pandemic had begun in the United States.

THE NEXT GREAT EPIDEMIC

The most important question raised by the 1918–1919 influenza pandemic is: can it happen again?

But the real question is not *if*—it is *when*? As much as scientists have learned about the causes, treatment, and cures of diseases in the nine decades since this global catastrophe, they still would stand effectively helpless in the face of a modern strain of disease as aggressive as the 1918 influenzavirus. Scientists still do not know how to prevent or cure influenza. And, while we are better equipped to fight the opportunistic diseases such as pneumonia that are the most frequent cause of death in epidemics, all it would take is the emergence of a single antibiotic-resistant strain of pneumonia or any one of a hundred different other diseases to spell disaster.

The fear of such a mutation in the influenzavirus already has epidemiologists losing sleep. In their January 2006 report "1918 Influenza: The Mother of All Pandemics," epidemiologists and influenza experts Dr. Jeffery K. Taubenberger of the Armed Forces Institute of Pathology and Dr. David M. Morens of the National Institutes of Health concluded "that since (the conditions that caused the 1918–1919 pandemic) happened once, analogous conditions could lead to an equally devastating pandemic."

There are many potential candidates for a pandemic, as the Taubenberger and Morens report warned: "Even with modern antiviral and antibacterial drugs, vaccines, and prevention knowledge, the return of a pandemic virus equivalent in pathogenicity to the virus of 1918 would likely kill more than one hundred million people worldwide. A pandemic virus with the (alleged) pathogenic potential of some recent H5N1 outbreaks could cause substantially more deaths."

The report noted that "in 2006, two major descendant lineages of the 1918 H1N1 virus, as well as two additional reassortant lineages, persist naturally: a human epidemic/endemic H1N1 lineage, a porcine enzootic [an epidemic in animals] H1N1 lineage [so-called classic swine flu], and the reassorted human H3N2 virus lineage, which like the human H1N1 virus, has led to a porcine H3N2 lineage. None of these viral descendants, however, approaches the pathogenicity of the 1918 parent virus."

Of particular interest to epidemiologists is the H5N1 strain, even though at present it requires physical contact with an infected bird for a human to catch the disease. There is no evidence that an infected person would be able to pass the strain to another person or transmit it through the air. It has, however, shown itself to be epizootic and panzootic (affecting many species over a large area) in bird populations, killing tens of millions and causing more than 100 million to be destroyed to contain the disease. It is often referred to as avian influenza or bird flu.

Of those humans who were infected by H5N1 in a 1997 Hong Kong outbreak, more than half of them died. The fear is that H5N1 will mutate or reassort into a strain that could be as easily and quickly transmitted to humans as its 1918 ancestor. Dozens of governments and private companies are developing vaccines to protect against H5N1's pandemic potential.

OUTBREAKS, EPIDEMICS, AND WARNINGS

Due to its nature, sudden mutations happen routinely in all strains of the influenzavirus, which is why—even alongside resurgences in such once-epidemic diseases as tuberculosis (a disease of the lungs whose symptoms include a persistent cough, fatigue, weight loss, night sweats, and fever and for which a vaccine has existed since 1927); measles (vaccine

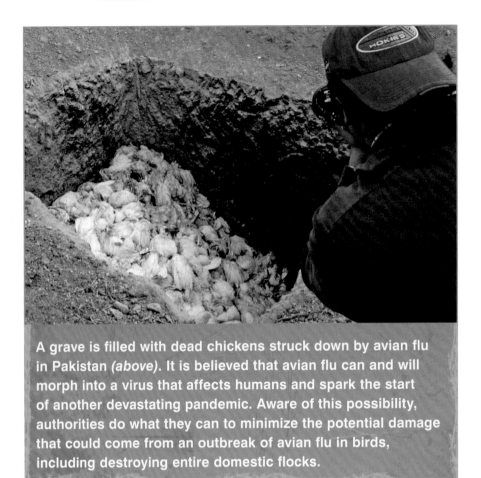

A grave is filled with dead chickens struck down by avian flu in Pakistan *(above)*. It is believed that avian flu can and will morph into a virus that affects humans and spark the start of another devastating pandemic. Aware of this possibility, authorities do what they can to minimize the potential damage that could come from an outbreak of avian flu in birds, including destroying entire domestic flocks.

discovered in 1963); and pertussis, or whooping cough (with a vaccine since 1926)—influenza remains high on the list of diseases to watch. In the United States, statistics are compiled and analyzed by the Centers for Disease Control and Prevention in Atlanta, Georgia.

In 1957, a pandemic of Asian influenza, a much milder strain than its 1918 counterpart, struck, killing an estimated 2 million people worldwide. It began in the Far East, even while health officials, expecting an outbreak and monitoring the world for them, began producing vaccine to protect against it.

The Centers for Disease Control and Prevention

The Centers for Disease Control and Prevention (CDC) located in Atlanta, Georgia, is a federal agency that was established in 1946 to coordinate disease control efforts in the United States and to serve as an intermediary and clearinghouse for disease control efforts and information worldwide.

The CDC, which has taken the lead in numerous public health crises, maintains research facilities specializing in the identification and eradication of disease. The CDC's Smallpox Eradication Program was responsible for wiping out that disease in the late 1970s, while its labs identified Legionnaires' disease as well as the 1993 outbreak in the southwestern United States of the previously unknown type of hantavirus, Sin Nombre virus (SNV). Hantavirus is a deadly disease transmitted through the infected bodily secretions of rodents that causes fever, chills, and respiratory distress.

Together with groups such as the United Nations's World Health Organization (WHO), created in 1948 in Geneva, Switzerland, the CDC coordinates international health efforts and information. It also promotes higher health, drug, and vaccine standards and creates guidelines for health and research. Essentially, the CDC stands on the frontlines of the war against disease.

The CDC has created guidelines to improve America's ability to identify infectious diseases and respond to them effectively. The plan's goals are:

(continues)

(continued)

* Surveillance, to quickly detect and rapidly identify emerging pathogens
* To combine laboratory science and field observations of the public to detect changes in health patterns
* The prevention and control of disease by communicating prevention strategies to the public
* The strengthening of the ability of public health providers at every level of local and federal service to communicate, support surveillance, and implement prevention and control strategies.

The virus was quickly identified and a vaccine made available by August 1957, well in advance of the start of the traditional influenza season. But in September, school began, and the virus worked its way through the school population, hastening the spread. In Britain, 50 percent of schoolchildren developed the disease; in residential schools, that shot up to 90 percent. Of about 30,000 deaths in England and Wales, more than 6,700 of them were attributed to the influenza itself rather than from pneumonia and other opportunistic infections.

The United States suffered 70,000 deaths from Asian influenza. The first wave, in late 1957, struck predominantly school-age children. The second wave, during January and February 1958, appeared to target the elderly, following a pattern where first one group of people is infected, followed by a decrease in infections in the first population, and then an increase in a different part of the population.

The Hong Kong flu pandemic of 1968 was an outbreak of the H3N2 strain of influenza, which caused more than one million deaths worldwide and nearly 34,000 in the United

States. Along with being a milder strain of the disease than the 1957 outbreak, the Hong Kong flu virus was similar enough to earlier viruses that had circulated between 1957 and 1968, providing wider immunity to the disease than previous strains. Also, the Asian flu struck in late December 1968, just before the Christmas holiday vacation in schools, which helped contain the spread. The same strain recurred in 1969, 1970, and 1972 but without the same intensity as the initial outbreak.

INOCULATION AND PREVENTION

In 1976, an outbreak of an H1N1 influenza at Fort Dix, New Jersey, was cause for widespread alarm. By the end of March 1976, President Gerald Ford, with the unanimous recommendation of the CDC, the Food and Drug Administration, and the National Institutes of Health, approved a mass immunization program. The virus was identified on January 27, 1976. The first doses of vaccine were shipped by September 22 and administered on October 1; by December 16, more than 40 million civilians had been immunized.

May 1977 saw the Russian flu scare, another H1N1 virus, first isolated in northern China, spread rapidly there through the population that was under age 20; most people older than that were likely to have developed immunity from exposure to the pre-1957 strain of the virus. A vaccine against the virus could not be produced in time for the 1977–1978 season, but it was included in the 1978–1979 serum.

The next big scare was the avian flu, first in 1997, sickening hundreds in Hong Kong and hospitalizing 18 people, of whom 6 died. Most bird influenzas have to first move through pigs before they change to affect humans. The 1997 strain jumped directly from chicken to man. To prevent the disease from spreading, the government had 1.5 million chickens slaughtered. Because H5N1 does not transmit easily between humans, the slaughter halted further human infections.

A 1999 avian influenzavirus, H9N2, only caused illnesses in two Hong Kong children, but its presence showed, once again, how quickly and easily the virus could mutate and adapt to infect humans. In 2003, avian influenza H5N1 hospitalized two in Hong Kong; also in 2003, an avian H7N7 strain caused 83 illnesses and 1 death, and an avian H5N1 caused 34 human illnesses and 23 deaths in 2004.

But it is not just new mutations capable of jumping to humans from the bird or animal populations that people

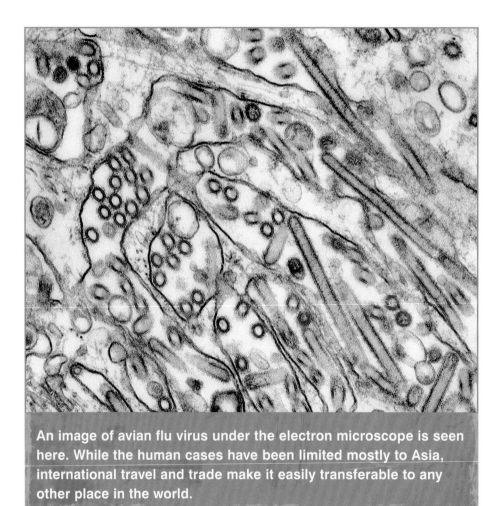

An image of avian flu virus under the electron microscope is seen here. While the human cases have been limited mostly to Asia, international travel and trade make it easily transferable to any other place in the world.

should be concerned with. In 2002, an old and familiar strain of the virus, H3N2, struck Madagascar, an island nation in the Indian Ocean off the southeastern coast of Africa. Prior to this, H3N2 was known for causing mild disease; this outbreak was anything but mild. An antigen shift in the virus led to a strain that caused an extremely high infection rate (as much as 67 percent of some towns) and a high death rate, before reverting back to its original status.

The World Health Organization's influenza centers stand at the forefront of monitoring and containing local outbreaks, but they are up against a difficult task because of the impossibility of accurately monitoring developing countries or convincing impoverished governments to use funds for flu research that they could use to buy food or treat the more immediate threats of AIDS and other diseases.

Yet even in the developed world, the attention of the research and preventive community is likely to be attracted by a more immediate, if not as deadly, threat, as in the case of the West Nile virus. West Nile virus is an encephalitis (affecting the brain) virus that mainly infects birds, small animals, horses, and humans and is transmitted to humans through the bite of an infected mosquito. In five years, West Nile killed fewer than 900 Americans. Yet more money was spent researching and preventing West Nile virus than on influenza, which sickens anywhere from 10 to 20 percent of the population, hospitalizes more than 130,000, and kills as many as 36,000 Americans each year.

Not only do we need to be concerned with new and more powerful strains of influenza but also with the speed at which it will travel through the population. In earlier times, pandemics traveled along sea-lanes by ship, spreading from continent to continent within a span of six to eight months. The 1918 pandemic, because of the unprecedented movement of troops around the world, moved at a much brisker pace, closer to the four to five months it took the 1957 pandemic to travel the world, while during the vastly more globalized 1960s, a pandemic made it from Hong Kong to the United States in about two months.

But if the disease is moving at a faster pace, so is the development of flu vaccines and medications. While once it took seven to nine months from the identification of an influenzavirus to the production and distribution of a vaccine (in the 1968 pandemic, vaccine became available one month after the outbreaks peaked in the United States), it is estimated that full-scale production of a vaccine against a particular strain would require three months from emergence to production, with one year needed to produce one billion doses. However, once inoculated, it takes about two weeks for adults and six weeks for children to acquire optimal protection against the viral strain, so by the time production, distribution, and inoculation can be achieved, the course of the disease may have already peaked.

Should the world face a pandemic today of the same magnitude as the 1918–1919 outbreak, the consequences would be, according to one WHO estimate, likely three times the deaths. There are today more than triple the number of people in the world than there were in 1918, and because pandemics only end when all the susceptible victims have either sickened, died, or acquired immunity through inoculation, the close to 7 billion people populating this world, in which no one is more than 24 hours away from any other point on the planet by airplane, provide a seemingly endless feast for an aggressive virus.

Research is ongoing, with new and more effective vaccines in development. Most vaccines are still produced using killed viruses, but a new, live-virus vaccine that can be inhaled was introduced in 2003. Also, the manner in which the flu vaccine is produced—cultures of the virus are injected into chicken eggs, where they multiply before being killed and extracted for the serum—is being looked at and perhaps molecular biological techniques can speed up the production.

People stood in line to receive the flu vaccine during a shortage in 2003 *(above)*. When the British government shut down a major manufacturer's plant, the United States found itself short by 50 million doses of flu vaccine. Warnings were issued the public that the healthy and able should refrain from inoculation, and the very young or elderly should receive the vaccine. This caused the public to doubt the government's claims of being prepared for the next flu pandemic.

The ultimate goal, of course, is a vaccine that would be effective against all strains of influenza by targeting the parts of the influenzavirus that all strains share in common.

The development of antiviral drugs is also a vital component in the fight against future pandemics. One such drug already in use is oseltamivir, which is effective against the H5N1 virus, although the H3N2 virus has shown the ability to develop a resistance to it.

We are almost completely unprepared for a new pandemic. As recently as 2004, there was a severe shortage of influenza vaccine for the coming influenza season. As much as science has progressed since 1918, we are still at the mercy of a single, random, genetic mutation that could unleash a modern-day plague every bit, if not more, terrible than the virus that swept the world in 1918.

Dr. Miner of Haskell County, Kansas, would be disappointed to see that things have not changed as much as they should have in the 90 years since his was the lone voice warning of the coming pandemic.

Chronology

1918 **January:** The first cases of a new strain of influenza appear in rural Haskell County, Kansas. Though it causes a high death rate, it is not high enough to cause alarm.

March 11: A private at Fort Riley, Kansas, reports to the infirmary with flu-like symptoms. By noon, 100 more are sick; by the weekend, influenza patients number 500. By June, this first wave of infection will have passed.

August 27: At a receiving ship at Boston's Commonwealth Pier naval station, sailors begin to report to the sick bay. Within days, more than 60 sailors are ill.

September 22: Approximately 20 percent of the soldiers at Boston's Camp Devens are sick with influenza. Despite the outbreak of a second wave of influenza, soldiers continue passing through this and other infected camps, picking up the infection for further spread.

October: On certain days during the month, cities experience staggering death tolls, including 202 in Boston, 289 in Philadelphia, and 851 in New York. It will be the pandemic's deadliest month, claiming more than 195,000 Americans.

November 11: World War I ends as the rate of infection declines. However, crowds taking to the streets to celebrate the war's end cause an upsurge in infections and deaths.

December: The pandemic's third and final wave begins with 5,000 new cases of influenza reported in San Francisco.

1919   **February–March:** In February, Paris had a death toll of 2,676 from influenza, with 1,517 more in March. For the same two-month period, Chicago and New York suffered 11,000 deaths. U.S. President Woodrow Wilson's wife falls ill in Washington; the president is stricken in Versailles, France. By the end of the month, the final wave passes.

Timeline

1918

January
The first cases of a new strain of influenza appear in rural Haskell County, Kansas.

August 27
At a receiving ship at Boston's Commonwealth Pier naval station, sailors begin to report to the sick bay. Within days, more than 60 sailors are ill.

March 11
A private at Fort Riley, Kansas, reports to the infirmary with flu-like symptoms. By noon, 100 more are sick; by the weekend, influenza patients number 500.

September 22
Approximately 20 percent of the soldiers at Boston's Camp Devens are sick with influenza.

1927   An American Medical Association study places the final death toll of the 1918–1919 pandemic at more than 21 million people worldwide. In years to come, that total will be revised upward, until a 2002 study estimates the number to be as high as 100 million.

October
It will be the pandemic's deadliest month, claiming more than 195,000 Americans.

February–March
In February, Paris had a death toll of 2,676 from influenza, with 1,517 more in March. For the same two-month period, Chicago and New York suffered 11,000 deaths.

1919   **1927**

December
The pandemic's third and final wave begins with 5,000 new cases of influenza reported in San Francisco.

An American Medical Association study places the final death toll of the 1918–1919 pandemic at more than 21 million people worldwide. In years to come, that total will be revised upward, until a 2002 study estimates the number to be as high as 100 million.

Glossary

adsorption   The attachment of one substance to the surface of another, as in the adherence of a virus to a host cell.

antibiotics   Chemicals that kill invading bacteria without damaging those that make up the body, usually by interfering with the cell's mechanism for building cell walls.

antibody   A protein substance produced by the body in response to the presence of a specific antigen that will reproduce and create millions of replicas to destroy the invading bacteria, usually by chemically breaking down their cell walls.

antigen   A foreign substance that causes the immune system to react and form a specific immune response.

antigenic shift   The combination of two different strains of influenza to form a new subtype that contains a mixture of the antigens from the two original strains; also known as reassortment or viral shift.

antitoxins   An antibody capable of killing a specific toxin; produced by the body in response to the presence of that toxin.

bacteria   A single-celled organism with a metabolism, requiring food, producing waste, and reproducing by dividing itself; some cause disease.

DNA   Deoxyribonucleic acid, a double-stranded molecule that carries genetic information from parent to offspring.

epidemic   A widespread disease that affects many individuals in a population, as in counties, states, or nations.

epidemiology   The study of public health and the factors that affect it.

four humors The four individual bodily fluids; ancient philosophers believed an imbalance caused disease.

immune system The various parts of the body that help to provide immunity from disease, including the lymphatic system, the spleen, and bone marrow.

immunity Resistance to a specific disease acquired from a prior exposure to that disease, usually through vaccination.

infectious Having the capability of spreading a disease.

inoculation The injection of a serum containing antibodies of a disease to confer immunity to that disease.

miasma Foul emanation from soil, air, and water that was once believed to carry and transmit disease.

mutation A permanent structural change to the DNA or RNA of an organism that often occurs at random.

pandemic A widespread disease that affects many individuals in larger populations, usually across international boundaries, often worldwide.

parasites An organism that feeds off another without benefiting or immediately killing the host organism.

pathogen Any disease producing a bacterium or microorganism.

pneumonia An inflammation of the lungs, which can have bacterial or viral causes and which causes fever, chills, and congestion of the lungs.

pulmonary Relating to the lungs.

serotype A group of closely related microorganisms distinguished by a characteristic set of antigens, or antibodies, present in the body triggers to fight off infection.

vaccine   The serum containing bacteria or viruses treated to give immunity to specific diseases.

virus   A DNA fragment wrapped in a protective shell that must attach itself to a living cell, injecting its DNA into the host cell's reproductive and life-sustaining machinery to reproduce itself.

Bibliography

Barry, John M. *The Great Influenza: The Epic Story of the Deadliest Plague in History.* New York: Viking Penguin, 2004.

———. "The Site of Origin of the 1918 Influenza Pandemic and Its Public Health Implications." *Journal of Translational Medicine*, published online January 20, 2004. February 11, 2007. URL: http://www.pubmedcentral.nih.gov/articlerender.fcgi?artid=340389.

Carruth, Gorton. *What Happened When.* New York: Harper & Row, 1989.

Centers for Disease Control and Prevention. "Biology of Influenza." Centers for Disease Control and Prevention Influenza Page. February 18, 2005. Available online. URL: http://www.cdc.gov/flu/keyfacts.html.

———. "CDC Influenza Pandemic Operation Plan." Centers for Disease Control Pandemic Operation Plan. March 9, 2007. Available online. URL: http://www.cdc.gov/ncidod/EID/vol12no01/05-0979.html.

Davis, Pete. *The Devil's Flu.* New York: Henry Holt, 2000.

Keen, Anthony. "Notes Prepared for Virology Lectures to Third Year Medical Students." University of Cape Town, Department of Medical Microbiology. February 18, 2007. Available online. URL: http://web.uct.ac.za/depts/mmi/jmoodie/influen2.html.

Taubenberger, J.K., and D.M. Morens. "1918 Influenza: The Mother of All Pandemics." Centers for Disease Control and Prevention: Emerging Diseases. April 3, 2007. Available online. URL: http://www.cdc.gov/ncidod/EID/vol12no01/05-0979.html.

Taubenberger, Jeffrey, et al. "Initial Genetic Characterization of the 1918 'Spanish' Influenza Virus." *Science* 1997: 1,793–1,796.

Thomas, Clayton L., ed. *Taber's Cyclopedic Medical Dictionary.* Philadelphia: F.A. Davis Company, 1975.

United States Census Bureau. "Special Tables of Mortality from Influenza and Pneumonia in Indiana, Kansas, and Philadelphia, Penn., September 1 to December 1, 1918." 1920.

Further Reading

American Experience-Influenza 1918. DVD. Produced by PBS. Directed by Matthew Collins and Rocky Collins. Narrated by Marion Ross, 2005.

Centers for Disease Control: CDC Influenza. Available online. URL: http://www.cdc.gov/flu/pandemic/cdcplan.htm.

Crosby, Alfred W. *America's Forgotten Pandemic: The Influenza of 1918*. New York: Cambridge University Press, 2003.

Getz, David, and Peter McCarthy. *Purple Death: The Mysterious Flu of 1918*. New York: Henry Holt, 2000.

Goldsmith, Connie. *Influenza: The Next Pandemic?* Ontario. Twenty-First Century Medical Library, 2006.

Health-Cares.net. "What Is Influenza?" Available online. URL: http://respiratory-lung.health-cares.net/influenza.php.

Iezzoni, Lynette. *Influenza 1918 (The American Experience)*. New York: TV Books, 2000.

Johnson, Niall. *Britain and the 1918–19 Influenza Pandemic: A Dark Epilogue*. London: Routledge, 2006.

Kolata, Gina. *Flu: The Story of the Great Influenza Pandemic*. New York: Farrar Straus & Giroux, 1999.

PandemicFlu.gov. Managed by the U.S. Department of Health and Human Services. Available online. URL: http://www.pandemicflu.gov/general.

PBS.org. "American Experience: 1918 Influenza." Available online. URL: http://www.pbs.org/wgbh/amex/influenza/filmmore/index.html.

World Health Organization. "Epidemic and Pandemic Alert and Response." Available online. URL: http://www.who.int/csr/disease/influenza/en.

WEB SITES

Centers for Disease Control and Prevention
http://www.cdc.gov

The National Institutes of Health
http://www.nih.gov

U.S. Department of Health and Human Services
http://www.os.dhhs.gov

World Health Organization
http://www.who.int

Picture Credits

Index

About the Author

PAUL KUPPERBERG is a writer and editor with more than a dozen books of nonfiction on topics including medicine, science, and history to his credit. He has also written novels, short stories, syndicated newspaper strips, Web animation, humor and satire, as well as comic, story, and coloring books. Paul is the executive editor of a national weekly publication and lives in Connecticut with his wife, Robin, and son, Max.